Praise for Claire McNear and

ANSWERS IN THE FORM OF QUESTIONS

"Claire McNear does a fantastic job capturing the spirit behind the *Jeopardy!* production team, fandom, and contestant
community. I already knew about a lot of this stuff, and I still
couldn't put it down."

— Brad Rutter, highest-earning *Jeopardy!* contestant

"I'd anticipated that reading a book about *Jeopardy!*—a game
show that has been in my life for basically all of it—would make
me feel a certain amount of nostalgia, and a certain amount
of warm joy. I had not, however, anticipated how sentimental
parts of it would make me feel, and how loudly other parts of
it would make me laugh. Claire has built something really great
here. I wish I could read this book again for the first time."

— Shea Serrano, #1 *New York Times* bestselling author of
Movies (And Other Things)

"Put this in your potpourri: Claire McNear has delivered
a treasure. ANSWERS IN THE FORM OF QUESTIONS
is a smart and sassy journey into the wide, wide world of

Jeopardy!—a must for anyone who's ever shouted out to Alex from the edge of their couch."

    — James Andrew Miller, #1 *New York Times* bestselling coauthor of *Live from New York* and *Those Guys Have All the Fun*

"Claire's book is the perfect way to learn more about what Alex Trebek and *Jeopardy!* meant to so many people and is perfect for any *Jeopardy!* fan in your life."   — The Jeopardy Fan

"As fast-paced and trivia-packed as the show itself…Anyone who has ever watched more than five episodes of the long-running quiz show has undoubtedly thought, 'I could do that.' While McNear's engaging exposé may quell such ambitions, it still provides fascinating and entertaining reading for devoted *Jeopardy!* fans."   — *Booklist*

"Packed with useful advice for aspiring contestants. Read this book and you can lose on *Jeopardy!*, just like me."

    — James Holzhauer, multiple-time losing contestant

"McNear lifts up the hood on *Jeopardy!* and shows us the inner workings, from quirky contestants and fans to details about the buzzer. I saw so many parallels to the Scripps National Spelling Bee too, from intensive and creative studying strategies through the decades to the balance between the live audience and the home audience. If you like *Jeopardy!* I highly R-E-C-O-M-M-E-N-D this book."

    — Dr. Jacques Bailly, official pronouncer of the Scripps National Spelling Bee

ANSWERS
IN THE FORM
OF QUESTIONS

ANSWERS IN THE FORM OF QUESTIONS

A DEFINITIVE HISTORY AND INSIDER'S GUIDE TO *JEOPARDY!*

CLAIRE McNEAR

FOREWORD BY KEN JENNINGS

New York Boston

Twelve
Hachette Book Group
1290 Avenue of the Americas, New York, NY 10104
twelvebooks.com
twitter.com/twelvebooks

Originally published in hardcover and ebook in November 2020

Trade Edition: August 2022

Twelve is an imprint of Grand Central Publishing. The Twelve name and logo are
trademarks of Hachette Book Group, Inc.

The publisher is not responsible for websites (or their content) that are not owned
by the publisher.

The Hachette Speakers Bureau provides a wide range of authors for speaking
events. To find out more, go to www.hachettespeakersbureau.com or call (866)
376-6591.

The Library of Congress has cataloged the hardcover as follows:
Names: McNear, Claire, author.
Title: Answers in the form of questions: a definitive history and insider's guide to
Jeopardy! / by Claire McNear.
Description: First edition. | New York: Twelve, 2020.Identifiers: LCCN
2020022710 | ISBN 9781538702321 (hardcover) | ISBN 9781538702314 (ebook)
Subjects: LCSH: Jeopardy! (Television program)
Classification: LCC PN1992.77.J363 M36 2020 | DDC 791.45/72—dc23
LC record available at https://lccn.loc.gov/2020022710

ISBNs: 978-1-5387-0230-7 (trade paperback), 978-1-5387-0231-4 (ebook)

Book design by Marie Mundaca

Printed in the United States of America

LSC-C

Printing 1, 2022

*For the couch shouters, the blind guessers,
the Coryat counters, the KHQA and
WXVT viewers, the Pavlov coiners, the pen
clickers, and Barrys and Berrys everywhere*

CONTENTS

FOREWORD

BY KEN JENNINGS

Jeopardy! is a magic trick.

It's been performed over eight thousand times, every weeknight for the last three and a half decades. But the trick goes off so smoothly every time that you never see the strings. You're probably not even aware that you're watching magic.

The show appears simple, effortless—even mundane, at this point. Its vast audience loves it for its straightforwardness, its utter lack of surprise. They get exactly what they expect every night: Alex Trebek, three contestants, roughly sixty answers and sixty questions.

But at home, you're seeing only a tiny part of the trick. It takes months of complicated preparation and a small army of people to produce a single half hour of *Jeopardy!* A lot of hard work goes into making television look this easy.

Let me warn you right now: In this book, you're about to see how the trick is done. Claire McNear is going to show you the strings. You'll time-travel back to the 1960s to be present at the show's creation. You'll be in the room with Alex Trebek at the crack of dawn as he spends hours poring over the day's games and clues. You'll follow the months of exhaustive nationwide searching that finds each set of three contestants.

You'll marvel at the bizarre training regimens to which the contestants may have subjected themselves, and learn what a surreal pressure cooker *Jeopardy!* gameplay is from the other side of the TV screen. (I still have flashbacks.)

If *Jeopardy!* is a sausage—and friends, I firmly believe that it is not!—you are about to find out how the sausage is made.

But here's the thing: The backstage *Jeopardy!* in this book is fascinating, but it isn't the real *Jeopardy!* I've noticed that the *Jeopardy!* diehards online sometimes forget that. They talk about the show as if it exists mostly to service superfans like themselves who know all the insider secrets—and who may very well be contestants themselves, either past or prospective. It's sometimes easy for me to forget as well, having not exactly been a *Jeopardy!* civilian myself for over fifteen years now.

But for the most part, all the behind-the-scenes trivia is beside the point. The real *Jeopardy!* is not the machine. It's the *show,* the thirty minutes of pleasant syndicated reassurance that the machine produces five times a week. *Jeopardy!* isn't in a chilly California soundstage; it's in your home, as you yell answers at the TV screen or furrow your brow during a tense Daily Double. Nine million people will enjoy it tonight, even if they have no idea that the show tapes five shows in a single afternoon, or what the *Jeopardy!* theme music is called, or what a "Coryat score" is. All that is gilding the lily. The real *Jeopardy!* is the illusion of simplicity: Alex Trebek, three contestants, roughly sixty answers and sixty questions.

The real *Jeopardy!* is the magic trick.

INTRODUCTION

In January 2020, the five most important figures in the history of modern *Jeopardy!* took the stage in a ballroom of the sprawling Langham Huntington resort in Pasadena.

The complex, with acres of manicured gardens, has served as a historic getaway for the entertainment industry's elite, and it drips with Hollywood history. The pilot episode of *Remington Steele* was filmed on the grounds, the building's exterior served as a playground for Lindsay Lohan's mischievous twins in 1998's *The Parent Trap*, and HBO's *Westworld* converted the hotel's lawn into a British Raj–styled theme park.

But few ever to visit the hotel can rival the iconic status of the group who made their way to a tightly packed row of gray director's chairs that winter afternoon.

On one end of the stage, James Holzhauer—who the year before had thrilled the nation with a thirty-two-game winning streak that saw him shatter record after record en route to becoming the fastest player in the history of the show to win $1 million—sported one of his signature V-neck sweaters and tight smiles. To his left sat Ken Jennings, with the ease and confidence that come with owning the all-time record for *Jeopardy!* victories thanks to a dominant seventy-four-game winning streak in 2004. They were joined by Brad Rutter—wearing a checked plaid suit purchased earlier after an ABC wardrobe consultant insisted on an emergency Nordstrom run for all three—a former record-store clerk who had set the record for the highest overall *Jeopardy!* winnings.

The trio had gathered in the room of television critics to promote their prime-time showdown—billed as the Greatest of All Time tournament—under the eye of the other two men on the stage, longtime host Alex Trebek and executive producer Harry Friedman. Having had some practice with the unusually high seats, both casually crossed their legs while the younger men dangled their feet awkwardly.

Friedman—just the third executive producer in modern *Jeopardy!*'s history—single-handedly dragged the show into the twenty-first century, pioneering a slew of major innovations, from doubling the prize money in 2001 to lifting the five-day cap for returning champions, which fundamentally changed the way the game was played. And with his long-planned exit from *Jeopardy!* just months away, the GOAT tournament would serve as a crowning achievement for a showrunner whose more than two decades on the job had been a persistent fight to broaden its pop-culture appeal while nurturing the bookish DNA that endeared the show to generations of nerds.

But the center of gravity—as it had been for the thirty-six years since he began hosting the show—was Trebek.

People might not have originally expected a smooth-talking, lightly sardonic Canadian to capture the hearts of American television audiences, but Trebek did just that with decades of knowing winks and gentle—okay, sometimes less than gentle—corrections of mispronunciations. For the show,

Trebek had been a constant unlike any other—a sometimes mustachioed, sometimes prickly, always steady presence, the keeper of a finite blue-purple world where the passage of time could be counted both in operatic ephemera and, maybe, the number of different living rooms where you found yourself watching over the years.

The assembled crowd engaged in a cursory discussion of the contest, asking how Jennings, who had won the previous night's opening round, and Rutter, who in twenty years of *Jeopardy!* competition had lost just a single tournament, intended to counter the newcomer Holzhauer, who had scandalized some viewers of the show with an aggressive playing style and betting strategy. The veteran contestants—who in reality had taped the competition a month earlier—talked about the ways they might tweak their strategies, noting that selecting from the middle of a category, rather than the top, improves your chance of hitting a Daily Double.

But the concern looming over the showcase—in fact, the reason it probably existed in the first place—was evident from a mere glance at the group.

Attached to the lapels of Holzhauer, Jennings, and Rutter was a purple ribbon—intended to promote pancreatic cancer research and a gesture of solidarity after Trebek's announcement a year earlier that he had been diagnosed with the disease.

Trebek, then seventy-nine, was asked about the outpouring of support he had experienced in the wake of his diagnosis, and he responded with trademark self-deprecation. He wrote off tributes to his decades of hosting as the type of recognition that anyone who had, like him, spent "more than half my life" hosting a program would receive. And he waved off accolades as a reaction to his illness.

"The pity factor is out there," Trebek said. "I'm not unaware of that."

His eye-rolling continued as critics asked the contestants to reflect on his role as host.

"Brad, James, and Ken," one reporter began. "The answer is: 'The thing you admire most about Alex.'" They would have to answer in the form of a question.

"Oh dear," quipped Trebek.

The panel concluded with more laughter, with Holzhauer commending the longtime host on navigating decades in Hollywood without embroiling himself in scandal.

"There's still time," Trebek responded.

But many of those gathered in the Pasadena ballroom—and millions of faithful *Jeopardy!* viewers across the nation—found themselves asking how much more time there might be before a show known as a beacon of television stability would change forever. As much as this was a moment of celebration for the show, it was also, perhaps, the end of an era.

Jeopardy! has achieved a rare omnipresence in American culture—befitting for the program that holds the trademark for "America's Favorite Quiz Show."

It's not merely its frequent appearances through cameos and spoofs on other television programs, though there have been many: from the *Celebrity Jeopardy!* and *Black Jeopardy!* sketches on *Saturday Night Live*, to *Golden Girls*, *Baywatch*, *The X-Files*, and *The Simpsons*, to the 2014 finale of *The Colbert Report*, in which Stephen Colbert rode off in a farewell sleigh alongside the foremost arbiters of American public life—Abraham Lincoln, Santa Claus, and Trebek.

With more than eight thousand episodes under its belt, the show has become a byword for brainy gumption: When 2020 presidential candidate Amy Klobuchar blanked on the name of Mexican president Andrés Manuel López Obrador, she later defended herself in a debate by saying, "This isn't like a game of *Jeopardy!*"

Indeed, no less than former Chief Justice of the Supreme Court Warren Burger once sent *Jeopardy!* a letter requesting that the show spotlight the Bill of Rights in a category in the upcoming season in honor of the document's 1991 bicentennial. Burger concluded his handwritten letter, "P.S. *Jeopardy!* is the only quiz show allowed in our home. It is truly a fine educational piece. Long ago Mrs. Burger and I were teachers." (The writers obliged the judge.)

Nearly four decades into its present incarnation, *Jeopardy!* has gained the patina of an immovable cultural artifact. At the 2015 Emmys, the comedian John Oliver joked, as he introduced an award for limited series, "Every show on television will go off the air eventually, with the sole exception of *Jeopardy!*"

Oliver continued, "And I'll tell you what: The sun could burn out, humanity could flee to another galaxy, time as we know it could cease to exist, but Alex Trebek will still be there scolding librarians from Ames, Iowa, to answer in the form of a question and passive-aggressively insulting their hobbies."

If it's felt like *Jeopardy!* has always been there, that's partly by design. "We came on the air very quietly, without any great fanfare," Trebek said in 2004. "There were no fireworks, no bright lights, no wild and crazy music. We were just an easy show to get used to, an easygoing rhythm."

But change is coming all the same.

Friedman, the EP, departed at the end of 2019–2020's Season 36 after a quarter century at the helm of *Jeopardy!* and fellow Merv Griffin creation *Wheel of Fortune*. Maggie Speak, the longtime head of *Jeopardy!*'s contestant department, also retired in 2020. A singular presence in the history of the show, Speak—who handpicked the contestants who appeared on each episode—did as much as anyone to shape the show millions of Americans watch every night.

As the GOAT tournament began to air, Trebek and his off-screen counterpart, announcer Johnny Gilbert, were well on their way to completing their fourth decade with *Jeopardy!*

But Trebek had been vocal about his grueling rounds of chemotherapy even as he continued to host. And that July, as the show wrapped its season, Gilbert turned ninety-two. That day in the ballroom, it seemed unavoidable that someday, perhaps even someday soon, the pair would hang up their signature blazer and bomber jacket.

A lot of change, in short, was due for a show Trebek himself once equated to "a nice warm bath."

"It is not known as a wild up and down show," Trebek said of the program. "There aren't these great highs and great lows. We just cruise along smoothly."

One thing, at least, is unlikely to change: the contestants.

Many fans are surprised to learn just how sportlike *Jeopardy!* can be. It has many of the hallmarks that we associate with sports: a prospect pipeline, rigorous physical (and, yes, mental) preparation, a hall of fame, and strategic innovators revered decades later for their additions to the game, who sometimes go on to assume the role of coaches.

The show's viewers, too, can take on a dedication rarely seen outside the confines of sporting fandoms. That's the way it is in the home of actor Michael McKean, where he and his family gather every night at 7:00 to watch the night's episode and play along, culminating in a nightly Final Jeopardy! showdown.

"There's only one rule—you don't talk about *Jeopardy!* club," he jokes.

No—it's something far more serious. Everyone stays silent through the first chorus of music during Final Jeopardy!, before counting down from three during the latter half and shouting their answers at once. (He insists that no one keeps track of their scores after the fact.)

McKean is admittedly no normal *Jeopardy!* fan: He's won *Celebrity Jeopardy!* on three occasions, and is, thanks to nabbing the grand prize in the 2010 Million Dollar Celebrity Invitational, one of just four *Jeopardy!* contestants ever to win a million-dollar tournament prize. (The others: Rutter, Jennings, and the IBM supercomputer Watson.)

The premise of *Jeopardy!* is simple enough: two grids of thirty questions, a preliminary round with a single hidden Daily Double betting opportunity and then the trickier Double Jeopardy! with two Daily Doubles, with difficulty and dollar value increasing downward. This is followed by one last question—Final Jeopardy!—on which players have the option to wager everything they have.

By the time a contestant makes it to the *Jeopardy!* stage, the odds are good that they have long been training in some form to compete on the show. Many players spend years working their way up through a series of nontelevised (and mostly nonpaying) circuits, a kind of Triple-A league for *Jeopardy!* hopefuls. Even casual viewers might be aware of the rise of advanced statistics on *Jeopardy!*, whose complex lessons about defensive gameplay, Daily Double and Final Jeopardy! wagering, buzzer advantage, and other metrics and tactics have fueled the rise of recent champions like Holzhauer.

A great *Jeopardy!* player is likely concerned with far more than just presidents, state birds, and the corresponding flash cards. That player may also have immersed themself in everything from game theory to thumb reflex and grip strength training and even, in some cases, scouting of other players ahead of time. On TV, you see a scant twenty-two minutes of action; for the contestants, those minutes may have been months or years in the making.

Before we get into it, some disclaimers. Most of this book will be concerned with the era that began with the show's revival in 1984 with Trebek and Gilbert. But today's *Jeopardy!* would not exist without the show's original incarnation on NBC, with actor Art Fleming as host and Don Pardo—later the legendary voice of *Saturday Night Live*—as announcer.

The original version premiered in 1964 and lasted (counting a one-season revival in 1978) twelve years. Unlike the modern edition, it aired during the middle of the day, making it and its lead-in *Hollywood Squares* a favorite of college students and workers on their lunch breaks.

The original *Jeopardy!* was also a hit, albeit of a different kind—at one point in its network-TV-heyday run, it captured a baffling 38 percent of the viewing audience—and one with some critical rule differences that we'll dig into later on. When Trebek first took over *Jeopardy!*, it was years before audiences were won over, and there still exist die-hards who refuse to watch the modern edition out of lingering loyalty to Fleming.

Without the success of the Fleming-and-Pardo *Jeopardy!*, there would never have been a Trebek-and-Gilbert *Jeopardy!* The show's endurance through the years is a testament both to Griffin's game as well as to the team that first wooed audiences into making it a daily routine.

My focus here will also be largely on the flagship *Jeopardy!* show, though the number of spin-offs it has spawned— including VH1's four seasons of *Rock & Roll Jeopardy!* with future *Survivor* host Jeff Probst, a sports-themed game hosted by former ESPN anchor Dan Patrick, and a children's version known as *Jep!* with Bob Bergen, the voice of Porky Pig—is proof of the show's seminal place in television history. That's true even outside the borders of North America: In 1996, 1997, and 2001, English-speaking champions from different nations' *Jeopardy!* franchises faced off in an International Tournament. (The winners: Sweden, Canada, and the United States.)

Another disclaimer: I am not a *Jeopardy!* contestant, former or, alas, future. I grew up, as so many have, watching the show with my parents, in awe of how the players (and—ugh— my parents) knew all this stuff. When I got an apartment (and a cable subscription, a few apartments later) of my own, recording *Jeopardy!* and shouting out the answers each night from the couch became one of my first traditions with my now-husband.

I started writing a column about the show as a fan—one largely unaware of how much goes on just beneath its surface. In time, I've come to know a bit about the depths of strategy and the world of contestants, both alumni and aspiring. My hope is to share some of that with you, so that wherever you count yourself within the *Jeopardy!* world—alum, future champion, or nightly shouter of answers from your own couch—you'll learn a little more about how the show works and what has made it such a unique corner of television.

As for my odds: I am a thoroughly lousy trivia player— a mediocre pub quiz participant at best. Even if I had the stomach for hand-to-hand, or brain-to-brain, buzzer battles on national TV—I emphatically do not—I know for a fact, as you will read in the coming chapters, that I won't be competing on the *Jeopardy!* stage anytime soon.

One additional technicality. *Jeopardy!* tapes most episodes approximately two months before they appear on TV; unless otherwise noted, episodes are referred to by their air date, not their tape dates.

With that: Let's meet today's contestants.

CHAPTER ONE

WELCOME TO *JEOPARDY!*

The shuttle arrives at 7:00 a.m. sharp, but on a Tuesday morning in Culver City, California, the hotel lobby begins to fill much earlier. One by one, *Jeopardy!* contestants start to gather around a table by the entrance. First a man in a suit. Then a woman in studiously neutral business casual. One contestant, who looks so young it's not clear if there's been some terrible Teen Tournament mixup, is accompanied by her father. He looks even more nervous than she does, which is saying something.

"Hi," an older man says as he hesitantly approaches the group. "Are you guys in the show, too?"

On taping mornings, it doesn't take much to figure out who has come for *Jeopardy!* Most sit beside overstuffed garment bags and backpacks containing a couple of changes of clothes—a requirement by *Jeopardy!*'s producers in case they make it to multiple episodes. The producers also ask that contestants iron their spare outfits ahead of time, but for many, well, there are bigger fish to fry.

And then, of course, there's all the studying. Flipping flash cards. Reciting First Ladies. Turning the crumpled pages of old compilations of clues past. Scrolling through inscrutable spreadsheets on laptops. Yes, the group in the lobby is in the show, too.

"I'm just practicing—no matter what Alex says, I'll say, 'That's right, Alex!'" says one.

"Just breathe," says another.

A third says that he heard one contestant is coming back from yesterday. "Someone *always* comes back from yesterday," a woman replies with dread. If the reigning champion is among them, they have apparently decided not to admit to it just yet.

Then, suddenly, a black van pulls up outside, and the driver walks into the lobby. A dozen pairs of eyes swivel his way, widening as they realize their ride has arrived.

"Guys," says the woman in business casual. "We're fine. We're *fine*."

One by one, the contestants stand, gather their bags, and head for the door. As the van rumbles away, headed for the famed Stage 10 down the road, the contestant's father waves and turns back to the hotel, looking like he very well might cry.

⟵

To understand *Jeopardy!*, you must first understand Charles Van Doren. In 1956, the Columbia University English professor appeared on the quiz show *Twenty-One*. Van Doren, thirty and boyishly charming, went on a tear, winning $129,000 over the course of fourteen weeks. At the time, quiz shows were huge—*The $64,000 Question* was the highest-rated show on television for the entire 1955–1956 season—and Van Doren was an instant sensation. Enthralled viewers followed the ever-growing heights of his streak night after night. While his episodes were on the air, Van Doren "received more than 20,000 letters (most of which he answered), was interviewed by about 500 newspaper men, [and] received several dozen proposals of marriage," according to a 1959 story in the *New York Times*.

But the problem with great stories, it turns out, is that they're not always true. *Twenty-One* and a handful of other popular quiz shows, including *The $64,000 Question*, manufactured the impressive runs of contestants like Van Doren by briefing them on the material prior to taping and occasionally by paying the episode's loser to throw the match. In the case of Van Doren (who would be played by Ralph Fiennes in Robert Redford's 1994 film about the controversy, *Quiz Show*), both methods were deployed. Van Doren claimed that *Twenty-One*'s producer promised him he would be the first-ever quiz show contestant to win $100,000, and he was.

The revelation of Van Doren's duplicity was front-page news in the *New York Times*, and so great was the public outrage that the federal government got involved. A grand jury investigation followed, and then a congressional subcommittee dragged Van Doren to Washington, DC, in 1959, where he confessed to the plot. Van Doren, who had at first professed his innocence, and nineteen other quiz-show contestants eventually faced perjury charges. President Dwight Eisenhower declared it "a terrible thing to do to the American people," and J. Edgar Hoover's G-men were said to have investigated the show-fixing beneficiaries for links to communism.

Congress took action, amending the Communications Act to state, among other things, that "it shall be unlawful for any person, with intent to deceive the listening or viewing public... To supply to any contestant in a purportedly bona fide contest of intellectual knowledge or intellectual skill any special and secret assistance whereby the outcome of such contest will be in whole or in part prearranged or predetermined." In the end, Van Doren and his fellow contestants escaped jail time—the judge issued suspended sentences, noting "how deep and how acute [their] humiliation has been"—and hung on to their ill-gotten winnings. But since 1960, rigging a quiz show—*a purportedly bona fide contest of intellectual knowledge*—has been a federal crime.

In the years after the congressional intervention, knowledge-based game shows understandably faltered. However pure producers' intent—now federally sanctioned—and however certain that contestants could now get by only on their genuine smarts, audiences and networks alike were spooked.

"Gee, I'd do anything to do a quiz show, but nobody will buy them because of the scandals," game-show impresario Merv Griffin remembered lamenting in the years after the scandal to his then-wife, Julann, in a 2005 documentary on *Jeopardy!*

She suggested creating a show that did exactly what was now prohibited: Give the players the answers straightaway. The twist, to make it legal (not to mention interesting), was that they would then have to work out the questions.

That's exactly what *Jeopardy!* did, debuting with host Art

Fleming in 1964—just four years after the new regulations took effect—with players ringing in with the iconic *What is…?* or *Who is…?* setup. *Jeopardy!*'s format is thus a deliberate nose-thumbing at the show-fixing scandals: If you give the contestants the answers up front, you can't very well be accused of doing it later.

Julann's idea, Merv would later write of his production outfit, Merv Griffin Enterprises, "took the company from the ground floor right to the penthouse."

While the day's contestants gathered at their hotel, Alex Trebek was already in the midst of his morning routine. Decades into his time as host, he arrived each morning at the Sony studio lot by 6:00 a.m. and settled in at his desk with a newspaper, crossword puzzle, and, more often than not, a Diet Coke. Breakfast long consisted of a chocolate bar—so great was his affection that the *Jeopardy!* staff once gave him a case of Snickers for his birthday—but in his later years he often reluctantly chose a granola bar instead.

Trebek liked to joke that he was sometimes ragged for not working hard enough, and in many respects, his was a cushy job. *Jeopardy!* tapes five episodes a day, two days a week, twenty-three weeks a year, from July to April—meaning that the venerable host headed to the office just forty-six days a year, taping a week's worth of episodes on each. For this, he was said to make north of $10 million annually.

Production days at *Jeopardy!* are long. By 7:30, Trebek would have a copy of the clues for all five of the day's games and would spend the next hour and a half at his desk, marking up each with diacritical annotations and consulting a dictionary for foreign names. Later, he would join the writers and a handful of producers for a final production meeting to go over the clues, with Trebek offering his own tweaks. The host made a point of trying to honor foreign tongues, breaking out elaborate pronunciations of everything from *genre* to *Die Fledermaus* to *Dracula* (a vaguely Slavic *Doorakula!*, no doubt as Bram Stoker intended). Once, apparently determined to stump him, the writers delivered Trebek a game that included a category called "When the Aztecs Spoke Welsh." He set about mastering the clues—heavy on the *L*'s and *X*'s, light on vowels—before someone finally pointed out that it was April Fools' Day.

Jeopardy! employs seven full-time writers and seven re-searchers, who together are responsible for 16,790 clues each season—the 61 that air in each game, plus 1 bonus clue per category prepared in case of a misfire. (Unlike the host, the writers and researchers keep standard nine-to-five hours, and they work substantially more than forty-six days a year, including during the show's annual summer hiatus.)

It's serious business—their decisions about what very smart people will find difficult will result in six figures' worth of IOUs (more on those later) being handed out by each tape day's end. But it's not taken *totally* seriously: Writing sessions begin with a ritual clanging of a cowbell, and—particularly in recent years—the subject matter tends toward the zany.

Not long ago, the writers uncovered a box of categories from 1984, the first year of the Trebek revival, and flipped through them, bemused by their scholarly simplicity: "Mammals," "Science," "History." Compare this with some more recent categories: "Weird Flex" and "But 'OK,'" "Key 'Key'" and "Do You Love Me?," or "I Can Haz Cheeseburger?" Clues are sometimes written for the amusement of *Jeopardy!* staff members: The words *spineless jellyfish* have appeared in at least seven games over the years, apparently because Trebek found the phrase funny. Once, in 1990, the writers built a Jeopardy! round where all thirty responses revolved around the name John: John Rockefeller, Olivia Newton-John, Lyndon Johnson, long johns, and so on. In a 2005 game, all but two responses were seven letters long, and the following year, every clue in a "Famous Treaties" category was looking for the answer "the Treaty of Paris"—except for the last, which asked for the treaty that ended World War I (the Treaty of Versailles).

As games are built, clues, which top out at seven lines of seventeen characters each, are color-coded: blue for academic subjects, pink for pop culture, yellow for wordplay, and green for items that don't fit easily into the other areas. For a Final Jeopardy! offering, designed to require a two-step thought process and written separately from normal *Jeopardy!* clues, to make it into the show, at least one fellow writer must know the answer. "I still can't wait to see how my categories will play during that day's shooting," writer Mark Gaberman once wrote of his job. "It never gets old."

Sourcing clues—in *Jeopardy!* parlance, pinning them—is pursued with journalistic rigor. Over the years, researchers have called everyone from Neil Armstrong (who said that a quote attributed to him was wrong), to the manager of the Kinks (who explained that there are indeed two versions of "Lola," thanks to the BBC's refusal to play a song that plugged Coca-Cola), to Tom Wolfe (who replied via handwritten fax).

"I work with the strangest, weirdest, funniest, smartest people," co–head writer Michele Loud said of the writers' room in 2019, "and we have strange, funny, weird, smart conversations that spark ideas that produce what you see on the game board."

That writers' room is a library on the Sony studio lot, filled with, among other things, several decades' worth of encyclopedias. In the pre-internet days, the writers and researchers ran the gamut of local radio contests, alternating which one of them would call in to answer the day's trivia: The odds were good that someone in the room would either know the answer or else have the necessary anthology handy. Colleagues joked that between the cash prizes and giveaways, Steven Dorfman, one of the show's original writers and the originator of "spineless jellyfish," earned a second income this way. A photograph of Dorfman, who passed away in 2004, hangs in the library to this day; Trebek said he was so prolific that the show is likely still using clues he wrote. "Even while he was being treated for cancer in the hospital," read Dorfman's obituary in the *New York Times*, "he was jotting down notes for possible *Jeopardy!* categories."

Staffers at *Jeopardy!* tend to stick around. "Working for *Jeopardy!* is an annuity," Trebek once joked. "You start and you go on forever." While that might not be exactly true, it's not far off. During 2019–2020's Season 36, a great many *Jeopardy!* employees were well into their second or third decade with the show. Trebek and announcer Johnny Gilbert, of course, had been there for all thirty-six years of the modern incarnation, as has announcer Johnny Gilbert. Harry Friedman, who announced at the season's start that he would depart the show in the spring, concluded his twenty-third year as the executive producer of *Jeopardy!* and his twenty-fifth at its sister show,

Wheel of Fortune. Co–head writers Loud and Billy Wisse joined in 1993 and 1990, respectively; Loud met her husband, segment producer Grant Loud, at the show, after he joined in 1997. Producer and senior contestant coordinator Maggie Speak joined the *Jeopardy!*-verse in 1995; stage manager John Lauderdale, an alumnus of *The Merv Griffin Show*, did so in 1985. Senior researcher Suzanne Stone has been pinning clues since the show's launch, and Glenn Kagan, another senior contestant coordinator, joined in just its third season. The show's two supervising producers, Lisa Broffman (who had already spent more than a decade at Merv Griffin Enterprises) and Rocky Schmidt, arrived in 1989 and 1985. (Schmidt, then working as a lawyer, won two games as a Season 2 contestant, and afterward left his job to become Trebek's assistant; he might have made Dwight Schrute proud when he at one point moved from assistant to the producer to assistant producer.) When it comes to *Jeopardy!*, anything less than a decade on the job marks you as a new kid on the block.

For many years, all *Jeopardy!* staffers were required to take the famously rigorous contestant test to be hired by the show. Once, when an ad for an open writer position attracted twelve hundred résumés, the show invited applicants to take the test in order to narrow the pool. The highest scorer, Kathy Easterling, was hired and ultimately created the show's (in)famous recurring category, "Those Darn Etruscans."

In his early years as host, Trebek made a point of taking the test annually himself. The *Los Angeles Times* reported that he once got a most respectable forty-three out of fifty. "Every morning when I wake up," he told a reporter in the '80s, "I look at my pillow to see if any gray matter has been leached out."

Unlike his predecessor, who made a point of expressing humility about the material—"If I didn't have that sheet in front of me," Fleming once told a reporter, "you wouldn't have found me within a mile of the studio"—Trebek was perfectly happy to let everyone know that his bona fides were the real deal. When Arsenio Hall made a crack on his talk show that Trebek wouldn't know any of the answers without the sheet in front of him, an incensed Trebek challenged him to a trivia contest. Sadly for audiences, if it happened, it was never televised.

⟵

The night before he went on *Jeopardy!*, Bruce Lou slumped into a chair by the bar at his hotel and sighed.

He'd spent the last twelve hours on edge. Today was supposed to be his day to play, but instead he'd gotten bumped to the following taping—*Jeopardy!* always brings in a couple more people than it needs, just in case. As a result, he'd spent the day at the studio watching other people compete. "That's a *champion*," he stage-whispered, pointing to a guy leaning against the bar and looking distinctly like he might fall asleep where he was standing while murmuring something about wanting a cigarette. Lou, twenty-two and still wearing the neat black dress shirt he'd hoped to make his TV debut in, ordered a Jameson on the rocks, and the server sheepishly carded him.

Lou got the call to come on *Jeopardy!* a month earlier. So fabled is this part of the contestant process that aspiring players sometimes style it as "The Call," and for Lou it arrived while he was in the middle of a meeting at work. He stepped out of the room. He thanked the producer. And then he went back in. "I had to go back to my meeting and pretend like nothing was going on," he says.

Lou grew up in Saratoga, California. He got good grades, got into a good college, graduated early, got a job at a tech company that let him live right in downtown San Francisco, made his parents proud. But now, one year into independent adulthood, it all felt a little lacking.

As a student, he'd done quiz bowl, the team trivia competition often found in scholastic settings, and won the National History Bee—a contest organized by David Madden, who was a nineteen-time *Jeopardy!* champion in 2005—and Lou found himself missing the competition. To Lou's parents, both immigrants from China whom Lou says are "pretty traditional," those extracurricular achievements had never really registered. "It's not grades," he said.

But there was one big exception: "They know *Jeopardy!*"

For Lou, *Jeopardy!* wasn't just another contest—it was an opportunity to win money, maybe a *lot* of money, perhaps even enough to do something else. Or to *be* someone else. A lawyer. A journalist. Who knows?

Within days of getting the call, Lou asked his boss for a leave of absence. By lining up all his vacation time, he arranged for three weeks away from his job to devote himself full-time to studying. He said nothing to anyone at work, much less his family, about why.

"I debated with myself—is it really worth taking off three weeks to prepare for this?" he said. But his mind was made up: "I'm not going to waste my shot."

Now here he was in Los Angeles, fresh from weeks of marathoning old *Jeopardy!* episodes and drilling himself on wagering scenarios and buzzer technique. (He practiced with the springy peg from his bathroom's toilet paper holder.) The day had been a misfire, but now he thought he had the lay of the land. And tomorrow, for sure, he would finally get his chance.

Each and every tape day, the player shuttle pulls up outside Stage 10—in 2021 formally renamed the Alex Trebek Stage— and a dozen new contestants spill into the bright morning sun. Many of them will be glad to break even: With the exception of tournaments, *Jeopardy!* doesn't pay for contestants' flights or hotels, meaning, among other things, that second- and third-place finishers from outside Los Angeles might end up using their entire $2,000 or $1,000 consolation prizes, respectively—or at least what's left of them after tax is accounted for—to pay for their journey.

The Wizard of Oz was filmed on this lot in the 1930s, back when it was still MGM HQ, and today an eight-story steel rainbow arches preposterously overhead in its honor. The lot, now Sony's, remains a busy place, and on any given day you might spot a curvy Ectomobile or the RV from *Breaking Bad* parked out front of a studio like it's no big deal at all. But before the players have time to take it all in—the supersize photo of Trebek, the giant *Wheel of Fortune* marquee on the soundstage next door—they are spirited inside to the green room.

Wheel of Fortune, which tapes on a set immediately adjacent to *Jeopardy!*'s, shares much of the same crew. On Tuesdays and Wednesdays, they rig the lights and monitor the game board on *Jeopardy!* On Thursdays and Fridays, they head across the alley—also recently rechristened as the Harry Friedman Breezeway, for the longtime EP—and do the same on *Wheel*. After the 2019 All-Star Games, the players and staff threw a party across the way at Stage 11 and took turns spinning the wheel.

It is here that contestants have long been swept up by the force of nature that is Maggie Speak—who, in case you were wondering, says she demolished All-Stars Brad Rutter and Leonard Cooper at *Wheel*. Fast-talking, razor-sharp, and quick to cut the tension with a laugh, she is, by virtue of being the primary decision maker as to who makes it onto the show, perhaps the most powerful person in all of *Jeopardy!*-dom. Speak grew up in Hollywood and began working on game shows while still a teenager. Eventually, she joined the short-lived children's version *Jep!* and the Jeff Probst–hosted *Rock & Roll Jeopardy!* before being snatched up by the mother ship, and there she has remained. Before retiring at the tail end of Season 36, Speak had been running *Jeopardy!* auditions for more than twenty years.

For many contestants, she is both the first and last person they will encounter in the *Jeopardy!* world, and at *Jeopardy!* events she is usually crowded by players, both former and aspiring, clamoring for a hug; she seems, however improbably, to recognize each, asking after new babies and demanding promises to say hello to absent spouses. In return, many contestants call her "Aunt Maggie."

On tape days, she and the other members of the contestant department not only read players in on the show, but also counsel them during and after their games. When *Jeopardy!* goes to commercial, a small pack of people can often be seen in the telecast descending on the contestants. Speak is usually among them, and she spends the duration of the break carpet-bombing them with pleasantries to keep them loose and counseling those who may have run into some sort of trouble: *You're a little early on the buzzer*, maybe, or *Try holding it this way*, or perhaps a plain old, *Take a deep breath, hon*—everyone is "hon" to Speak—*you've got this.*

Traci Mack, who taped in late 2019, felt nothing but confidence as she prepared to play. That changed the moment she stepped onto the stage for her game and, as she waited for the theme song to start, suddenly found herself in the grips of a full-blown anxiety attack. "Maggie came over to me," she says, "and just hugged me and talked to me about my daughter until I calmed down."

Speak "makes a lot of jokes," says Mack. "And she shows you a shirtless picture of Alex Trebek."

JEOPARDY!'S BIGGEST LOSER

According to Andy Saunders of the blog *The Jeopardy! Fan*, 26.25 percent of contestants between September 2003 and November 2019 won at least one game—meaning that 73.75 percent of contestants lost their very first game. Losing, in short, is a fact of life on *Jeopardy!*

But it's one thing to lose, and quite another to lose badly. Just ask Heather Chapman.

Chapman was in labor when her cell phone rang. Desperate for something to take her mind off childbirth, she answered, and on the other end was

Maggie Speak, asking if Chapman could come on *Jeopardy!* in three weeks. "I thought I was high," Chapman says. "I thought there was something in the epidural."

And then, pumped up with endorphins, she said yes. Speak—by then aware of what was happening on Chapman's end—asked if, given the circumstances, she was sure she wanted to do it.

"I remember thinking, *Oh man, this my chance*," says Chapman, who had already auditioned once before and not heard back. *"They're never going to call me again."*

Three weeks, one birth, many diapers, and not a lot of sleep later, Chapman traveled from her home in Lexington, Kentucky, to Los Angeles with her mother in tow. Hers was the last game of the day, against Martin Truong and defending champion Dan Pawson, who would finish with a nine-game winning streak and win the following year's Tournament of Champions.

Things started to go wrong for Chapman almost immediately. She saw that the categories weren't ones she knew well: geometry, Catholicism, weapons. But she knew she had to try, and she buzzed in over and over, wrong more often than right. The worse things got, the more aggressive she knew she had to be, and ten times she rang in first, only to guess the wrong answer. She lost $2,000 on a Daily Double. Once, she even forgot to start an answer with the requisite "What is...," leading Trebek to chide her.

Chapman's final score: negative $6,200—at the time, a record for the worst performance ever. (Patrick Pearce's negative $7,400 from July 2021— a game that happened to feature returning champion Matt Amodio at the beginning of his 38-game winning streak—is the current record. An honorable mention goes to Joan Kantor, who came in at negative $5,100 in 1985, when clue values were half what they are today.) Players who finish Double Jeopardy! with a negative score aren't allowed to participate in Final Jeopardy!, and so, not even twenty minutes after the chaos began, Chapman was led to a chair just offstage to watch as her two opponents finished the game without her, feeling, she says, "the weight of hundreds of eyes" on the back of her head.

After the game, Chapman, who was awarded the third-place prize of $1,000, and her mother left the studio. "We went to a Starbucks down the street and I just started sobbing," says Chapman. "When it's something you've wanted to do your whole life, and then it goes that badly—not just regular bad, but epically bad?"

The tears kept coming, and she felt a hand patting her on the back. "I thought it was my mother at first," she says, but gradually realized it was someone else—a stranger, apparently homeless, sharing the

Starbucks patio. "He kept saying, 'It's going to be okay, whatever it is.' And then I felt like the biggest jerk in the world, because what are my problems compared to this guy's?"

The loss had been embarrassing enough, she says, but perhaps worse was knowing that it would be on TV for everyone to see a couple of months later. The night her episode was set to air, she and a friend went to a local bar—in search, Chapman says, of "a little Dutch courage"—and had a server tune one of the TVs to *Jeopardy!* Gradually, the people around them caught on and started sending shots her way. "Desperate times, desperate measures," she says.

Chapman has heard that in the years since her game, Speak has mentioned her in pregame orientations as a proud example of a contestant who went down swinging. "I don't know if I would recommend that strategy," says Chapman, laughing. "But I appreciate the sentiment."

In the end, she got some game-show redemption: In 2019, Chapman won $20,000 on *Who Wants to Be a Millionaire.*

Before they play, players are first given a crash course in showbiz. In the green room, they're touched up with makeup and walked through the basics. You may not swear. You may not wager $69 or $666. And, for the rest of the day, you may not go to the bathroom by yourself.

While popular memory of the 1950s quiz-show scandals may have faded, the federal law prohibiting trivial skulduggery has not. As a result, *Jeopardy!* maintains a rigid division between contestants and all those who work with the clues. It's not just the writers who are siloed from players: So too is the host, whose review of the clues each morning effectively rules out any mingling with the day's contestants, given they know what awaits them in their games.

As a result, the grand total of time that most players get with the host is what happens on-screen during their episode, plus the moment it takes to pose for a photo onstage—one they're reasonably likely to use as their profile picture on social media for the next decade or three. In Trebek's case, the first question former contestants got was almost always something about him: *What was he really like?* Thank Van Doren for the fact that the host remained an enigma. And thank him, too, for the fact that the *Jeopardy!* staff doesn't let contestants roam the set. If you've gotta go, you're escorted to the facilities and straight back.

Eventually, contestants are led three by three to the stage, where someone—usually Jimmy McGuire, a member of the globetrotting Clue Crew that provides on-location video clues—stands in as host of a mock game, which exists purely for players to get a handle on the buzzer.

By this point, contestants have had ample time to size one another up, identifying those they absolutely do not want to face: the ones who nailed the buzzer every time they rang in during the practice game or who not-so-subtly let slip that they won a collegiate quiz bowl title. Then there's the small matter of the returning champion, who has been peeing under surveillance for at least a day now and perhaps looked just a little too comfortable on the green room couch.

On this day, Mike Upchurch is lounging on the couch, too. Like Lou, he came to the studio the day before and got bumped to the second round of taping. Unlike Lou, who is eager to study the fresh batch of competition, Upchurch relaxes next to reigning two-day champion Aaron Goetsch while the producers walk this second group of players through the same policies he heard the day before, with Speak spiritedly mimicking Trebek's Canadianisms—"Oh, soo-rry" is a favorite—just as she had the first time.

Upchurch, forty-eight, says he had wanted to be a contestant for as long as he could remember, but it never seemed like something that might actually happen. "Well, sure, I want to be on *Jeopardy!*" he remembers thinking. "I want to be an astronaut, too."

After years of taking the online test, he was finally invited to an audition in the fall of 2019. Two weeks later, as he and his wife were—what else?—watching *Jeopardy!* at home in Chicago, Upchurch glanced at his email and saw a message from a producer asking him to call back.

Now here he is on the set for the second day in a row. A few days earlier, he'd woken up in the middle of the night, suddenly desperate to remember the capital of Hungary. "Then when I remembered it," he says, "I was like, well, shit, now I need to remember the capitals of Romania and Serbia and Croatia and the Czech Republic and Slovakia..." Sleep, in short, had been hard to come by.

He initially found his fellow contestants intimidating. "Something like this, a bucket list item, you can't help but feel a little bit of impostor syndrome," he says. "Sitting in the green room I heard a lot of 'I have a PhD' and 'My wife's a PhD candidate' and I heard Stanford and I heard Berkeley.

Even more intimidating were the ones who were not even thirty. I'm like, what have I done with my life?"

But sitting in the audience and silently playing along the day before, he realized that it was the same old game he'd been watching since, as he puts it, he was "a bumpkin in North Carolina." By day two, he was ready.

When it's time to play, all the day's contestants are led into the studio audience.. The *Jeopardy!* studio fits about 160 people, but all is not as it seems on TV. The right half of the audience facing the stage (that is, stage left) is filled with contestants waiting to be called up for their game. Their plus-ones—spouses, parents, friends—are seated in the left half along with any civilians who've snagged tickets, which are free and generally spoken for within minutes of release.

Contestants are given strict instructions not to acknowledge, or even so much as look at, their guests while they wait for their turn to play. "My family would just loudly proclaim things knowing that I could actually hear them," says Mack. "Like, 'Well, I hope *Traci* knows that...' My family is not the kind of family who would be quiet."

During high-stakes tournaments like the All-Star Games and 2020 Greatest of All Time tournament, the public is replaced by *Jeopardy!* staff and network executives to prevent spoilers. On a normal day, though, there are no binding nondisclosure agreements for audience members— the only thing stopping them from spilling the beans before the episodes air is respect for the institution. Call it dork solidarity.

The champion and the first two challengers, whose names are called at random, take their places behind the lecterns.

Behind each is a hydraulic lift meant to raise shorter contestants so that all three players seem to be the same height on camera.

These are a relatively recent innovation: When five-foot-one Pam Mueller played six-foot-six Frank Spangenberg in 2005's Ultimate Tournament of Champions, she stood on a stack of three boxes, while producers joked about removing a floor panel and having Spangenberg play in a hole. "In the old days when I first went out there," remembers Spangenberg, who says he feels for those who've had to play next to "a big galumphing guy" like him, "it really was a wooden box."

Spangenberg holds a rather unusual *Jeopardy!* distinction. While post-taping spoilers from the audience are exceptionally rare—the clip of thirty-two-time champion James Holzhauer's 2019 loss to Emma Boettcher, for example, leaked in video form the night before it aired, suggesting it came from an affiliate station and not from the audience members who witnessed it in real time months earlier—that's not always the case. News of Ken Jennings losing his seventy-fifth game leaked just after it taped in 2004, so when he returned for the first time to play in the Ultimate Tournament of Champions the following year, producers were extra cautious. As a result, Spangenberg, who was called in as an alternate for the finals match among Jennings, Rutter, and Jerome Vered, might be the only person who's ever had the *Jeopardy!* audience all to himself.

With the three players ready onstage, the producers and judges take their seats at the long table to the left of the set. It's finally time to play.

THE WORLD ACCORDING TO
FRANK SPANGENBERG

It took the Grand Canyon to finally convince Frank Spangenberg that things might not ever go back to normal.

He was hiking along the South Rim when a woman cleared a nearby ridge, exposing her to the winding siena gorges he had been traversing.

"Oh my God!" she gasped. "Oh my God!"

Spangenberg nodded, taking in the splendor of the canyon himself—until the woman clarified what had her so impressed.

"Oh my God," she said again. "You're Frank Spangenberg!"

Says Spangenberg, resigned, "It's better to be known as a *Jeopardy!* champion than to be known as an ax murderer."

When Spangenberg—whose imposing stature, New York twang, and thick handlebar mustache (he maintains it to this day) make him easily identifiable—turned up on the *Jeopardy!* sound-stage in September 1989, he wasn't so much in search of glory as trying to give his co-workers a break.

He was just beginning his career with the Transit Police (now Transit Bureau) in Brooklyn, working steady four-to-twelves (4:00 p.m. to 12:00 a.m. shifts). Every night at 7:00, the officers would switch on *Jeopardy!*, each chipping in a quarter and giving the pool to whoever got Final Jeopardy! right. Spangenberg won so often that his fellow officers soon refused to play with him.

"Instead of taking our money," a colleague told him, "go take theirs."

Spangenberg, who retired as a lieutenant with the New York Police Department in 2020, did, and then some. He amassed a record $102,597 in five days (the five-day limit for returning champions had not yet been removed). That record, when multiplied by two to reflect the 2001 doubling of dollar values on the board, remained unbroken from its 1990 airing all the way until April 2019, when James Holzhauer finally surpassed it during his own first five days on the show.

Spangenberg, who turned sixty-three in 2020, quickly became a fan favorite. He was, perhaps, *Jeopardy!*'s first viral contestant, even earning an appearance on *Late Night with David Letterman*, where he played the *Jeopardy!* home edition with the host.

Spangenberg has since returned for five tournaments, most recently the 2014 Battle of the Decades; after he won 1993's 10th Anniversary Tournament by naming the playwright Wendy Wasserstein, Wasserstein invited him to dinner. "She said that her family and friends made more of a fuss about her being a Final Jeopardy! answer than they did about her winning the Pulitzer Prize," he once re-membered, "and she wanted to meet the man who knew her name."

The game has evolved since Spangenberg first laid waste to it, and he confesses he's not the biggest fan of the Holzhauer-ian style of board-hopping. "I understand why he does it, but I'm very old-school," he says. "But I'm delighted that he did well.

"There is no other show quite like it," Spangen-berg adds of *Jeopardy!*'s endurance through all these years. "You might as well ask why the Super Bowl is popular."

Talk to just about any *Jeopardy!* contestant and they'll tell you the same thing: The twenty-two-odd minutes that it takes to tape an episode are just about the fastest of your whole life.

Nearly forty years in, *Jeopardy!* is a well-oiled machine, and delays are few and far between. As a result, the show often tapes in scarcely more than the time it takes to play on tele-vision, and many players find that their memories of playing are a blur of bright blue.

In the control booth, director Clay Jacobsen sits in front of a wall with some fifty different feeds and camera angles, displaying everything from the untouched game board to contestant close-ups to the screens where their names are written. Unseen by players, it's Jacobsen who's calling the shots, starting with this very first one. There's a countdown from five, and Jacobsen gives the order: "Announce!"

Gilbert, seated behind his own lectern beside the judges' table and listening via headset, does as he's asked. With the magic words—"And here is the host of *Jeopardy!*, Alex Trebek!"—the host at last emerges from backstage, diving straight into the day's first game in what is usually the contestants' first glimpse of him.

In one of the longtime *Jeopardy!* announcer's only nods to being in his nineties, Gilbert adopted the practice of skipping the three games filmed in the morning, arriving after lunch for the final two of the day and back-taping the welcome for the ones he missed. Which means that in episodes airing on Mondays, Tuesdays, and Wednesdays, Trebek's ritual acknowledgment of him—"Thanks, Johnny!" or the occasional "Thank you, Johnny Gilbert!"—was actually delivered live to an offstage stand-in, often Sarah Whitcomb Foss of the Clue Crew. The announcer has been a frequent subject of clues over the years ("Johnny lent his skills to both the 1950s version & the current Bob Barker version of this show." What is *The Price Is Right?*) as well as their occasional reader. "Fiddle-dee-dee!" he exclaimed in 2013. "War, war, war; the war talk's spoiling all the fun at every party this spring." (What is *Gone with the Wind?*)

The first game of the day had just ended when Upchurch heard his name called and made his way to the stage. He had just watched Lou win the morning's opening game, a bruising match against reigning champ Goetsch and Mandy DeLucia, a restaurant consultant from Newport Beach, California.

Lou's weeks of prep had paid off. He led for most of the game and found all three of the board's Daily Doubles, even getting up to what Trebek himself called "a commanding lead." Having committed ahead of time to playing aggressively, he did exactly that. On the first Daily Double, he went all in and missed. On the second, he bet $3,000 and again missed, this time letting out an "*Oof!*" On the third, with $7,800 in the bank, Lou bet $5,000 and was right, finally giving him a chance to celebrate—he mimed draining a three-pointer à la Steph Curry, prompting an "Okay!" from a surprised Trebek.

As Double Jeopardy! concluded, Goetsch, realizing that Lou had finished with a runaway score and locked his fellow players out of contention, turned to Lou and told him, "Good job." Lou nodded and smiled fleetingly, then looked serious again. He still had Final Jeopardy! to get through and then: the next game.

A few minutes after Lou's first game ended—all three players missed a Final Jeopardy! clue about Pope Benedict XV's *Maximum illud* letter, but Lou had bet cautiously enough that it didn't matter—Upchurch and a third contestant, Kim Lutz, joined Lou onstage for the second game of the day, with Upchurch now taking the middle lectern. That morning, Upchurch remembered, Lou had flitted around the green room with the busy energy of a hummingbird. "I don't think Bruce ever sits down," he said.

But before Upchurch had much more than a moment to think about how to counter him, Lou reappeared from backstage in a new dress shirt, and took his place on the far right—the champion's lectern.

Before setting off for LA, Upchurch received *Jeopardy!*'s wardrobe instructions—the extra changes of clothes, plus a warning against bright white and busy patterns like plaid, which read poorly on camera—and realized his work as a writer had left him at something of a disadvantage. "I work from home, so 90 percent of my wardrobe has drawstrings," he says.

His wife, Carol, embarked on a thrift-store mission, returning with a bag stuffed with so many options that Upchurch joked that he packed for his trip like a diva.

The day before, he had woken up in his hotel at 3:00 a.m. and, unable to fall back to sleep, paced his room—there was no way he'd learn anything new before the shuttle arrived, he figured, and he could at least try to keep his new outfit from getting wrinkled while sitting around. Now he found himself onstage in a black blazer and a button-down (a getup, he says, that was "Carol-approved")—and then, there it is, *this—is—Jeopardy!*, and Trebek once again strolled onto the stage.

Backstage, the show's game board operator, Michele Lee Hampton, sat before the miniature grid she uses to manually pull up each and every clue onto the onstage board, listening through a headset and then tapping into the blue square as Upchurch found the first Daily Double of the game. Already $200 in the red, he deadpanned that it was "perfect timing."

"Perfect timing indeed," said Trebek. Upchurch got it—simple exercise routines derived from the Greek words for beauty and strength are "calisthenics"—and Lou whipped around and applauded. This time, the buzzer was giving him trouble: At the first commercial break, Lou had just $400, with Lutz to his far left at $1,600 and, in between them, Upchurch leading with $3,600.

"Now, it says here that you met your wife at a four-day heavy metal music festival," Trebek—*Trebek! Right there in front of him!*—said to Upchurch. "How do you engage a person in conversation at a"—he paused to enunciate the words again—"*heavy metal* music festival?"

Before they play, contestants prepare a notecard with a handful of anecdotes for this portion of the episode. The contestant coordinators highlight the ones they think might work best and deliver them to the host. Trebek occasionally liked to go rogue. When he sent the show off to its first commercial break, the host would gather the notecards and, meandering off-camera to where the three contestants nervously awaited him, flip through them for the very first time.

This kept his reactions fresh, and his occasional shock at what he found there authentic. "Your favorite type of music is something I've never heard of, but it doesn't sound like fun," Trebek said to Susan Cole in one 2016 episode. Cole gamely explained the premise of nerdcore hip-hop, prompting the host to furrow his brow. "*Losers*, in other words," he said of her fellow nerdcore fans. (Cole didn't seem particularly rattled—she won that game and the next two as well.)

In the fleeting, frantic, mid-game moment under the lights, suddenly face-to-face with the legendary host, more than a few contestants found themselves embellishing or outright manufacturing their tales. Just remember: *That's right, Alex.*

Upchurch recounted the tale of meeting Carol: "I feel like the fact that she couldn't hear a word I said or even get a good look at me really worked to my advantage," he quipped, and the audience laughed.

BREAKING THE *JEOPARDY!* NEWS

Every morning at 7:30, Dave Ross watches *Jeopardy!*

While many *Jeopardy!* viewers think of the game show as an evening affair, that's not the case everywhere. Because the show is syndicated, television stations are free to schedule it whenever they like, and its time slot varies across the country. On some stations, it airs before *Wheel of Fortune*; on others, it airs after. According to Matt Carberry, a *Jeopardy!* fan who has analyzed affiliate data, just under half of the 210 stations that carry *Jeopardy!* air it at either 7:00 or 7:30 p.m. local. The rest run the gamut: In Chicago, for example, *Jeopardy!* airs every day at 3:30 p.m.

Montgomery, Alabama, long carried the nation's earliest airing at 9:30 a.m. CT, a full hour and a half before any other station in the country. (For fans really wanting to impress their friends, that left eleven hours between the end of Final Jeopardy! and the moment when the same show would begin airing in Los Angeles—plenty of time to catch a flight for anyone hoping to pull off a real-life Bill-Murray-in-*Groundhog-Day* spectacle.)

So for Ross, who lives in Las Vegas and deployed a streaming tool set to Montgomery's affiliate station two hours ahead, that is when he would watch, tuning in before he'd even had breakfast and becoming among the very first viewers in the nation to learn the day's *Jeopardy!* outcome.

As you've probably guessed, Ross, sixty, is no normal fan. He is known in *Jeopardy!* circles as

"Jay"—"Boy, I probably just picked it almost completely at random," he says of the nickname—and provides a singular utility to the show's most devoted followers. Nearly every weekday morning since 2013, as the Montgomery episode was wrapping up, Ross published a recap online, breaking the news to the world of the day's new champion.

Spoilers on a show like *Jeopardy!*, where a staid middle manager winning a few games would count as big news in many months, are admittedly something of a niche concern. And Ross, for his part, isn't actually trying to ruin the result for those hoping to learn it on their own later in the day. Ross's ambitions are grander. "I'm essentially looking for some of the aspects of the show that the show itself never discusses," he says.

Those aspects principally include wagering—how much a player risked on a Daily Double or in Final Jeopardy!, where they stood among their opponents at the time, and how it worked out for them—and he views it as an educational endeavor. He polls his readers on whether they knew the last clue, hoping to gauge whether it was a particularly tough one, and long cataloged what he called "this day in Trebekistan": any unusual musings by the host. "Alex called 1917 a 'good year,'" Ross noted in his writeup of the April 29, 2020, game. "I can only assume he thinks that because the National Hockey League was formed in November of that year." There is, says Ross, precisely no money in the recaps.

"This recap—one of the goals of it is to get people to think while they're watching the show, what would I and what should I do in that situation," says Ross, "so that when they actually are on the show, it won't seem like such a mystery. They'll be ready."

Ross has been watching *Jeopardy!* nearly all his life. Now retired after a career as a financial planner, he remembers coming home for lunch during elementary school and watching the original Art Fleming version of the show, which aired at noon. "It's been something I've dealt with practically forever," he says.

Ross says that he has taken *Jeopardy!*'s online application test "pretty much every time they've offered it"; in 2020, he got his first-ever invitation to an audition. But on this—and on whether he is now in the contestant pool, and thus a candidate to appear on the show himself—he is mum.

As of 2021, Ross's station of choice had moved *Jeopardy!* to a later time slot; the nation's *Jeopardy!* newsbreakers now tune in to either KHQA in Quincy, Illinois, or WXVT in Cleveland, Mississippi, at 10 a.m. Pacific, the new earliest airing. For Ross, it is at least an opportunity to sleep in.

The game resumed and Upchurch kept pushing as his lead grew: He had $8,000 heading into Double Jeopardy!, with

Lou at $2,600 and Lutz at $2,200. But as Double Jeopardy! began, Lou found the buzzer's rhythm once again. He got the round's first clue, then the second, then the third—five straight right answers and suddenly *he* was in the lead. Lou again found a Daily Double, bet $5,000, and was right (Angel Falls is the waterfall that former Venezuelan president Hugo Chávez declared should be known by its indigenous name, Kerepakupai Mera); as the round drew to a close, he found the third one, too. With $20,000 in the bank and a $6,800 lead over Upchurch, he decided not to risk it and wagered just $3,000. He was right once again, identifying "the Good Samaritan" as the helpful figure in the Gospel of Luke.

"You're not missing the Daily Doubles today," Trebek observed—half an hour or so after "yesterday."

Lou entered Final Jeopardy! with $23,000, with Lutz trailing at $9,000 but Upchurch and his $15,600 too close for comfort. The stage lights glowed their customary red as the question, in the category "Children's Books," loomed: "This book was published in Latin as *Virent Ova! Viret Perna!!*"

It helps to be playing from a couch in the present time line, where, two months after taping, Dr. Seuss's birthday had been just the day before the episode aired. Lou couldn't work out the Latin to get to *Green Eggs and Ham*—instead, he wrote "What is...I hope I won." (Helpfully, the *Jeopardy!* staff ensures that players don't lose via a missing *What is* or *Who is* on the last clue by instructing them to write the relevant interrogative during the preceding commercial break.)

But Upchurch figured it out, and he bet big: $11,000. As the credits rolled, Trebek approached the contestants and asked Upchurch—now the new champion, with a total of $26,600—

if he'd been sure that he had the right answer. As Upchurch explained how he'd gotten there, Lou looked down at his feet and took a deep breath.

In a daze, Lou was led off the stage, taking the three big, blue-illuminated steps down from the glassy floor of the *Jeopardy!* set to the normal one of the real world. Meanwhile, Upchurch found himself ushered back to the green room, a handler plucking off his microphone as he went.

There, Upchurch was given the rapid-fire instructions that await any freshly crowned *Jeopardy!* champ: Change into your next outfit, sit back in the makeup chair to be touched up, and—hurry now!—then there will be another escorted trip to the bathroom.

"I have never had to pee so often in my life," says Upchurch of the sudden onset of what he calls *Jeopardy!* bladder. "It was like my body was telling me: *Get rid of everything so you can run! Your life is in danger! There's a dinosaur chasing you, and you need to run!*"

Swarmed by the myriad staffers who make the show run on schedule, there was little time for reflection. "I don't think I stopped talking between the two games," Upchurch says. "Honestly, all I was doing was trying to make them laugh to take my mind off what had just happened so I wouldn't shit my pants, because I couldn't process it."

For years, Trebek spent the fifteen-minute gaps between games taking questions from the audience. *Was he offended by Will Ferrell's impersonation of him on* Saturday Night Live? Hardly; he loved it. *What does he do in his spare time?* He likes to tinker around the house, and recently remodeled his wife Jean's bathroom. (Or else: Drink Chardonnay.) *Who does he think should be the next host of* Jeopardy!? Why, Betty White, of course. *How would he do as a contestant?* He might be able to get by—but only in a tournament for senior citizens.

He sometimes used the time for more serious matters. While taping his episodes in November 2018, at the height of the special counsel probe into possible collusion between the Trump campaign and Russia, onetime champion Charbel Barakat remembers the host solemnly breaking actual news to the contestants, who had been separated from their cell phones all day.

"During a break in the action, instead of taking questions, Alex put on his best Walter Cronkite voice and rumbled," Barakat recalls, " 'Ladies and gentlemen, I regret to inform you that after a lengthy, rambling press conference, the president has fired the attorney general.' Gasps filled the room."

In the intro to his second game, Upchurch beamed as his name was read and shook his head like he couldn't quite believe that $26,600 was his—like he was already imagining telling Carol, back home in Chicago, all about it.

He again led heading into Double Jeopardy!, but his opponents, Margaret Beaton and Paul Trifiletti, mostly boxed him out in the second round. By Final Jeopardy!, he was in third, and even delivering the correct answer—the twentieth-century artist whose name meant "savior" in Spanish was Salvador Dalí—could only push him into second place.

Trifiletti—who himself would create a moment of micro-virality when he incorrectly guessed that Philadelphia 76ers star Joel "The Process" Embiid's nickname was "Do a 180"—won instead, with a total of $21,000 in what would end up being the first of five victories. (Embiid jokingly embraced the alternative nickname on social media, and even referenced the incorrect guess weeks later when applauding Sixers

management for abandoning a controversial plan to imple-
ment salary cuts during the coronavirus pandemic. "In these
trying times, I'm proud of the Sixers organization for reversing
course and 'doing a 180,'" Embiid tweeted.)

And so Upchurch found himself on the other side of
the process he'd just experienced. Suddenly, it was all about
the champion—unclipping Trifiletti's microphone, scheduling
Trifiletti's bathroom break. For those whose *Jeopardy!* jour-
neys have come to an end—that is, the, er, nonwinners—
they are taken backstage, given a flimsy pink form listing the
amount they'll be sent a check for after their episode airs,
handed a tote bag and a *Jeopardy!* baseball cap, and sent on
their way.

＿

Jeopardy! invites players to stick around in the audience after
their last game and keep watching. Understandably, given that
a player's last game is the one that ends with a loss, many
don't. Upchurch went straight for margaritas with the friends
he'd brought along to the taping, a plan they'd agreed upon
in advance: "I figured if I embarrass myself, I'll go and get
shitfaced," he says. "And if things go really well, I'm still going
to go get shitfaced."

For those who fell in their first game up, joining the robust
ranks of one-and-done *Jeopardy!* contestants, they're often
eager to get out of the studio as quickly as possible.

"I disassociated from my body," Barry Petchesky, an editor
at the website *Defector*, says of his game in 2009, when he
came in third. Invited to stay and watch the next game—
which is to say, to stay and watch the person who just beat

him keep playing—he demurred, instead taking a cab back to his hotel with the player who came in second, Inta Antler. (Antler, who had won the game before that, generously paid for the ride, says Petchesky.)

While *Jeopardy!* doesn't pay for contestants' passage to LA, the show has a discounted rate at the nearby hotels that the morning shuttle stops at, so that's where most players stay. The result is that those hotels can sometimes feel a bit like a dorm during freshman orientation, with players propping their doors open and mingling with the competition. Another result: The bar scene on Tuesdays and Wednesdays is something to behold.

A couple of hours and a nap after his return, Petchesky made his way down to the hotel bar. There he found his green room cohort, many just returned from the studio. In all, it was about a dozen people, most of them, like Petchesky, crushed about losing on the game show they'd spent so much time trying to get a place on, with a buzzing handful who had, just as suddenly, won a great deal of money. All recovering from near-deadly levels of cortisol; all rejoicing in not yet having to keep the secret of how the day went, as they would with friends and family back home, in the couple of months before their episodes would air.

"The winners were just putting down their credit cards," says Petchesky, who adds that he witnessed at least one impromptu coupling in his group. "It felt like an old movie—I think someone actually said 'This round's on me!' and gestured to the whole room.

"Everyone felt like they'd been through the wars together," he added.

A few hours after Lou's loss, he still couldn't stop thinking about where he'd gone wrong. The morning's nervous dad and daughter had strolled back into the lobby, she in her new *Jeopardy!* cap and both looking giddy, followed by a parade of the others, all clutching their commemorative tote bags and looking vaguely shell-shocked. Lou came in last, the shirt he'd changed into back in the green room now untucked and a little rumpled. After his loss, he'd left the studio and gone to Venice Beach—he was in LA, so why not? "I looked so out of place," he said, "wearing a shiny formal shirt and dress shoes. It seemed so surreal, like a dream."

Now back at the hotel, the day was turning in circles. Why didn't he bet more on that last Daily Double? Why didn't he work out *ova*? Why did he ring in if he was going to say that Westphalian was a kind of *apple*? "I don't know if I'll celebrate," he said. "I could have done better." He swallowed hard.

Jeopardy!, he knew, was over for him—there are no invitations to reunion tournaments for onetime champions. As that reality began to set in, he ricocheted between despair—he had trained as hard for this as he had for anything in his life and still lost—and something else: not happiness, not yet anyway, but something like acceptance.

Everyone else on the *Jeopardy!* stage had been like him, he realized—had wanted it just as much as he did. Win or lose, he said, "we're all the smartest person that everyone around them knows." There was something strange and special about sitting in that green room. Even Madden, the nineteen-time champ, reached out to congratulate him.

Lou's winnings—$13,000 and change—were nice, but unlikely to reroute his life. The next day, he would drive back to San Francisco, and the day after that, he would go back to his job, where his boss remained none the wiser about what he'd been up to. Two months later, he would host a watch party at his apartment, friends filling the room to watch as he was crowned champion—even a girl he met at a bar the weekend before and convinced to come watch his television debut. Lou had always been shy and mortified by the idea of public speaking. But there he was on national TV, sailing through the board, whiffing on those first Daily Doubles and then pulling himself right back up again. "How do you know that?" his friends kept asking.

This, though, still waited down the road—he still had to go back home, to a world of people who had no idea what had happened in the *Jeopardy!* studio.

He paused to think about what he would do about the looming mystery. "I won't tell work until it's close to the air date," he said, and then smiled. "Then I'll tell people to watch one show, and then that's it—that's *Jeopardy!* I won!"

CHAPTER TWO

DO YOU KNOW THE STUFF OR NOT?

I'm perched on the edge of an empty pink Jacuzzi tub, and the temperature in the room is steadily rising.

It's the opening night of perhaps the most hallowed weekend in competitive trivia: Trivia Nationals. Every summer, hundreds of the nation's best and brightest descend on Las Vegas to face off in brainy events. There are ones you've probably heard of—quiz bowl, a spelling bee, a souped-up pub quiz—and many others you might not have: a not-quite-scavenger-hunt called Not-A-Race, a *Jeopardy!*-esque, buzzer-based competition called 5x5 (pronounced *five-by-five*), which has an even more challenging five players instead of three, and something ominously called Smush.

This year—2019—many attendees have come for one event in particular: *Jeopardy!* announced it would hold an in-person audition for anyone interested, and there are, to put it mildly, a whole lot of anyones interested.

Contrary to what the Trivia Nationals name would seem to suggest (or that of its precursor, the Trivia Championships of North America, or TCONA), there isn't much in the way of a competitive circuit in adult trivia. There are, for example, no qualifying regional events to make it to the national program: All you have to do is buy a ticket and follow the trail of bookish people with lanyards around their necks straight past the Tropicana casino—where Les Folies Bergere once danced and Siegfried & Roy first debuted their big-cat act, where *The Godfather* filmed and no less than Sean Connery's James Bond declared the accommodations "quite comfortable"—to the sterile conference rooms around back. But while there might not be an admissions test to get there, it's a distinctly self-selecting crowd.

Among the hundreds of people who show up each summer, there are an astonishing number of successful game-show contestants and collegiate quiz bowl champs, some perhaps just a little too eager to relive their glory years. Not that there's much in the way of prizes. The top scorer in most events walks away with a medal, while one event awards a pair of glitter-bedecked jeans: the literal smarty pants. It's a tight-knit community with a quizzical verbiage all its own: for starters, YEKIOYD ("You either know it or you don't"), WECIB ("What else could it be?"), and RTFQ ("Read the fucking question").

The arrival of the *Jeopardy!* team has kicked the perennial spectacle into overdrive. Members of the show's contestant department wander the halls, and the newly promoted co–head writer, Michele Loud—who is usually kept safely out of reach of players desperate for intel—is set to appear on a panel alongside Maggie Speak and a handful of champions.

Fritz Holznagel—a five-time *Jeopardy!* contestant who first appeared in 1994—is scheduled to run a seminar based on his 2015 book, *Secrets of the Buzzer*, a manifesto of sorts on buzzer technique that took on cult status after James Holzhauer credited it as the key to his own success with the dreaded signaling device. The weekend is, in short, an aspiring *Jeopardy!* contestant's dream come true.

With the audition looming a couple of days hence, many of those signed up are seizing the opportunity to brush up on their skills, piling into a suite to play board after board of simulated *Jeopardy!* games. While a hotel room should in theory offer some refuge from the August desert heat, the air-conditioning is no match for the sheer number of people crowded inside. They sprawl out across the floor, the bed, every chair; they lean, like me, against the enormous Jacuzzi tub and try not to think about what else this room, with the in-hotel wedding chapel just downstairs, has seen. Someone jokes about trying out the in-room sauna for relief. No less than Speak herself pops her head in, shakes it, and leaves.

The games are played via a complex rig hooked up to the television. At its center is a small black box, from which extend five buzzers designed to mimic the ones on *Jeopardy!* (The same gear will be deployed in the 5x5 competitions later in the weekend.) The games themselves are written by Trivia Nationals attendees, some of them past champions, who take turns standing in as host and reading the clues while another person furiously works to operate the bright-blue "board," using a laptop to cue up each called clue in *Jeopardy!*'s classic white Korinna font. (A bit of trivia: The same typeface—

which is named for the circa-sixth-century BC Greek poet—was used for text on *Frasier* and in the music video for Devo's "Whip It." Max Miedinger, who created the font used in *Jeopardy!*'s category names, Swiss 721 BT, is better known for another typeface: Helvetica.)

Makeshift though the system might be, the backroom games—a favorite unofficial event each summer—run smoothly. Apart from the extra players, the simulated matches play out nearly exactly like the real thing, Daily Double laser sounds and all, and as such offer just about the best practice anywhere outside of Culver City. This is little surprise to most of those playing: The simulator—the work of a onetime 1995 champion named Bill Schantz—is the stuff of legend.

Schantz first started building the simulator in 2000 to help some friends train for a *Jeopardy!* audition. At the time, says Schantz, there were *Jeopardy!* home and video games on the market, but none that offered a realistic version of the gameplay, particularly when it came to the buzzer.

So Schantz, a computer programmer by trade, designed his own. His earliest simulator featured PVC pipe buzzers wired to a deconstructed keyboard, and in 2005 he introduced it to the *Jeopardy!* public at the Game Show Congress, another precursor to Trivia Nationals.

As Schantz has coded ever better—and ever more *Jeopardy!*-like—versions, contestants in training have turned to him to get in reps before they hit the stage. Russ Schumacher and Alex Jacob, winners of the 2004 and 2015 Tournament of Champions, respectively, both sought out Schantz and his simulator to help them train.

Schantz was called on again ahead of 2019's All-Star Games, a new tournament in which prominent *Jeopardy!* champions drafted other past winners for a team-based competition. Buzzy Cohen, the 2017 Tournament of Champions winner, and his selected teammates—Jacob, as well as 2015 Teachers Tournament champion Jennifer Giles—visited Schantz in Denver and played a marathon fifty-five games over the course of a single weekend. They trained, jokes Cohen, at altitude.

"All three players from the *Jeopardy!* Greatest of All Time tournament have played the simulator at one time or another," Schantz says.

In the Tropicana suite, one player goes for a true Daily Double and the room, like so many studio audiences before it, gasps; when a competitor offers "*A* Winter's Tale" instead of "*The* Winter's Tale," a fierce debate breaks out over the importance of definite and indefinite articles.

A player hoping to get a shot in the next round mentions that one year, Colby Burnett—winner of *Jeopardy!*'s 2012 Teachers Tournament and the subsequent Tournament of Champions, a historic twofer—joined to read all the clues for one game. "That was *soo* cool," he says.

Many a *Jeopardy!* alum is present at Trivia Nationals. This year, an attendee might catch glimpses of—and perhaps even face off against—Burnett, then-six-time (now-seven-time) contestant and all-time winnings leader Brad Rutter, 2017 Tournament of Champions runner-up Alan Lin, and Pam Mueller, a five-time contestant who first competed in the 2000 College Championship, which she won. In what might have been their first-ever face-off, Rutter and Holzhauer—known here colloquially by many as Jamie—once battled it out in Las Vegas in a round of Knodgeball, hurling dodgeballs at one another as they simultaneously shouted the answers to trivia questions. Rutter won.

Many, many more *Jeopardy!* vets roam the halls, which at times have the feel of an alumni reunion or Trebek fan convention, complete with stick-on heart tattoos that say ALEX in the middle. During one session later in the weekend, past *Jeopardy!* contestants would be asked to gather for a picture, prompting nearly half of those in the sprawling ballroom to stand. When the speaker asked how many of the remainder were planning to audition later, every other hand shot up.

Events like Trivia Nationals function as an informal feeder system for *Jeopardy!*, which can generally be thought of as the pinnacle of the trivia world. (That sentence would surely have sent a chill down the spine of Merv Griffin, who was said to hate the term *trivia* for its air of unseriousness and wanted it far away from *Jeopardy!* Fortunately for us all, *Jeopardy!*'s writers resisted.)

Though there is both harder trivia (for example, the online, invite-only trivia serial LearnedLeague) and more openly competitive trivia (quiz bowl, not to mention much of the programming at Trivia Nationals), there is no trivia so well regarded or, maybe more important, so widely known. For decades, the show has served as a cherished proving ground for smart people to show the world that they are just that.

The reasons for *Jeopardy!*'s primacy skew sentimental as well, thanks to the show's longevity. Many adult bookworms nurse memories of awkward childhood years when their burgeoning intelligence made them feel geeky or strange or otherwise *other*, and when they perhaps discovered the steady run of *Jeopardy!* as an early outlet—something to watch over lunch with a kindly teacher, or something where the precocious delivery of answers illuminated for a family member, maybe for the very first time, that their little brainiac was destined for greatness. Other game shows offer the chance of fortune and maybe even a hearty fifteen minutes of fame. But on American television, only *Jeopardy!* offers the potential for brainy validation.

As a result, getting onto the show has become a matter of obsession for more than a few trivia die-hards. Matty Kimberlin, forty-three and a stay-at-home dad, is one of them. As a child, he remembers his father competing on *The Joker's Wild*. In the years since, he has made numerous visits of his own to game-show stages, appearing on *Win Ben Stein's Money*, *Whammy!* (a short-lived reboot of *Press Your Luck*), and *Who Wants to Be a Millionaire*. "Unfortunately, so far I've won a grand total of $1,000," Kimberlin says.

But it's *Jeopardy!* that he really wants a shot at. "I mean, it's the Holy Grail of game shows," he explains. Kimberlin—who would take home the weekend's "smarty pants" award, wrapping the jeans up in plastic in the quixotic hope of keeping the glitter from coating everything he owns—has taken the contestant test fourteen times. Prior to Las Vegas, he had a single invitation to an in-person audition to show for it—one that did not result in being picked for the show.

A few years ago, frustrated by his failure to advance, he decided to formalize his preparations.

"I set up a spreadsheet where every night I religiously marked my score and how I was doing," he says. From this, he identified weak points and developed a study plan— something that led to trivia discoveries of his own, which he deployed in a *Jeopardy!* game he wrote and hosted on Schantz's simulator.

He and his wife are now in the process of starting a trivia business, hoping to build a roster of bars that use their questions quiz night after quiz night. These days, he watches *Jeopardy!* at home with a practice buzzer he bought one year in Las Vegas, the better to master the timing for when, or if, he gets a chance on the real thing.

Kimberlin says that all these years of preparing for *Jeopardy!* might have been for the best. "It's one of those things where it's really a blessing in disguise, because as much as I say, 'Oh, I wish I had been picked for auditions earlier'—well, not really, because I wasn't as good then. So maybe now I have a better chance at winning a few games."

For Kimberlin, *Jeopardy!* is alone among game shows. "There's no wheel, there are no Whammies. It's really just a matter of: Do you know the stuff or not?"

KEN JENNINGS TAKES THE STAGE

It had already been a long morning for Bruce England when he stepped onto the shuttle that would take him from his Culver City hotel to the *Jeopardy!* studio one day in the spring of 2004.

For England, it was the second day in a row of this routine. The previous morning, he'd woken and made his way to the shuttle, where he grabbed a seat beside a nice young man named Ken, whom England noticed had brought along more changes of clothes than any of the other contestants.

"I mistook his very earnest demeanor for naïveté,"

says England, "and thought to myself, *I can beat this kid*."

Once the shuttle reached the studio, England learned just how wrong he was. A contestant coordinator broke the news: The nice young man's last name was Jennings, and he had so far racked up $1,321,660 over the course of thirty-eight victories. England taped in April, he says, two months before Jennings's episodes would begin to air. *Jeopardy!* had only lifted its five-game limit for returning champions the year before; prior to Jennings, exactly three players had surpassed it, with the longest spree lasting all of seven days. Jennings's streak was so outlandish that it seemed impossible. He was just getting started.

And so England spent the rest of the day in the *Jeopardy!* studio audience, watching as Jennings knocked off contender after contender, swiftly adding five more victories—not to mention $110,801— to his record. England was sent back to his hotel to get his chance to play the following day.

Knowing what awaited him, he slept poorly, and it is here that I should probably say how England introduced himself to me. "I'm the guy he"—Jennings—"mentioned in *Brainiac* who smoked pot before heading to the studio," said England.

In 2006, Jennings published *Brainiac*: part *Jeopardy!* reflection, part deep dive into the world of trivia. In it, he mentions some of the players he met during his *Jeopardy!* streak, including a man who admitted to him that he had just smoked two bowls of weed in order to relax. "It must have worked— during our game, he seems *very* relaxed," wrote Jennings.

England tells me that he's smoked pot since the 1970s. It became his evening routine: He would get high, go for a swim, and then watch *Jeopardy!* He kept track of his score, and was pleased to find that being stoned had no effect. Why mix things up when he finally got his chance to play?

Except for that frightful first day in the studio. The morning of the second day of taping, England woke up early from a strange dream about the *Jeopardy!* prompt "What is granite?"

"That morning I smoked two bowls instead of one," he says. "The argument *could* be made that that was one bowl too many."

Indeed, the game did not go well, at least for him. He blew a question asking him to alphabetize "Snap, Crackle, Pop" by, er, not alphabetizing them. He mistook George Clooney as Rosemary Clooney's son, not her nephew. He and fellow challenger Dana Dolan struggled so mightily to beat Jennings on the buzzer, England says, that the show was sent to an early break after just ten clues so that contestant coordinators could take a moment to coach them. England even let the time run out on a $2,000 clue that asked for the building material in use at Massachusetts's Pilgrim Monument: granite.

In the end, he finished with a score of negative $4,800—the largest deficit of any of Jennings's opponents—with Dolan in second place at $3,999 and Jennings waltzing on to game no. 45 with another $45,000 in hand.

Jennings would make it a baffling thirty more games before real estate agent Nancy Zerg toppled him in his seventy-fifth game. His streak, with episodes spanning six months and winnings totaling $2,520,700, was nothing short of a cultural phenomenon. Ratings leapt 50 percent from the previous year to an audience of fifteen million, and as he closed the season midway through his run with thirty-eight wins to return again in the fall, *Jeopardy!* was the second-ranked show on television after *CSI*.

The elimination of the five-game limit wasn't simply an act of generosity by *Jeopardy!*: It was a deliberate ploy by the show to beef up ratings. Perhaps producers had envisioned that such a move would allow audiences to get more invested in players and root for those with ongoing streaks—both of which happened. But it's hard to imagine that they foresaw that it might allow the show to introduce new *characters*, slowly building a pantheon of long-streaking, oft-returning champions who have changed the way viewers watch *Jeopardy!*

Jennings's streak was also responsible for the creation of the online database J! Archive. With viewers suddenly desperate for detailed breakdowns of the latest games, a small band of dedicated fans joined forces to build the first version of the website, taking over where an earlier version called the Jeoparchive had left off. Two of the J! Archive's original archivists are still active today: Robert Knecht Schmidt, who became a *Jeopardy!* champion in 2010, and Andy Saunders, who also runs *The Jeopardy! Fan*.

All through the summer and fall of 2004, the archivists worked, tracking down old episodes and screencaps and building out the site's back end in preparation for the J! Archive's official launch— which ended up happening, coincidentally, the very day that Jennings lost to Zerg.

Today, the J! Archive is an unparalleled resource in the *Jeopardy!* community. Its database contains details of nearly every episode in the show's history, which are painstakingly logged, clue by clue, by a team of volunteers. As a result, it's the go-to source for *Jeopardy!* history both big (Jennings's post-streak tournament record: one victory and four second-place finishes) and not-so-big: In the July 5, 2000, episode, Johnny Gilbert, apparently tied up by the return of then-two-day champion Glen Savory, introduced Trebek as "Glen Trebek."

The J! Archive is also, by virtue of being the unofficial record of just about every answer and question in the history of the show's answers and questions, a critical tool for those studying to appear on the show. That group includes the research team at IBM, which would, a few years after England's rough day in Culver City, look at Jennings's game data and try to figure out how to beat him with their new supercomputer: Watson.

Every year, about a hundred and twenty-five thousand people take the online *Jeopardy!* contestant test. A passing score—generally thought to be thirty-five out of fifty possible correct answers, though the show declines to specify—means an invitation to an in-person audition. Of the roughly twenty-five hundred people who make it to an audition, where they take another fifty-question test and then participate in a practice game and brief Q&A in front of the show's producers, only four hundred or so will get the call to come on that season to compete.

The odds, in short, aren't great, even if you have the wits to pass the online test. Consider that Holzhauer, who averaged a smidge north of a single wrong answer in each of the thirty-three games in his historic winning streak, took the online test thirteen times and auditioned twice before he made it to *Jeopardy!*

(The show might have some reason to be cagey about what getting through it entails: In the early years, when the show was upfront about the thirty-five-out-of-fifty bar, players would sometimes call to complain about being shut out. One irate applicant, who had scored well but been dismissed by a contestant coordinator, called Trebek himself to make his case. Trebek intervened and he made it on—and entered Double Jeopardy! with negative $3,400.)

Other storied contestants have also had long waits: Roger Craig auditioned three times before finally getting the call, and Rutter himself was turned down in a College Championship search. That applicants never know for sure if they passed the test, or what it would even take to pass—though many gather afterward in places like the *Jeopardy!* subreddit and the forum JBoard to compare responses, hoping for some numerical certainty—makes them a maddening experience for many *Jeopardy!* hopefuls.

But Vegas offered a loophole. Interested parties could effectively bypass the online portion of the application process and skip straight to the audition, where they would then have to take a similar test. If they passed—this time, they would know for sure—they would be invited to a practice game later in the day and, in theory, enter the *Jeopardy!* contestant pool. (At normal *Jeopardy!* auditions, applicants do take a second test but continue on to the practice game without knowing if their result has already doomed them. No pressure!)

The deal I had struck with the producers was that, in exchange for keeping the text of the clues, which are sometimes used in multiple auditions, to myself, I could sit in on the day's events, a fly on the wall to the entire audition process. While would-be contestants ground their teeth in front of the producers, I would be safe behind my notebook.

The morning of the audition, a jumpy crowd gathered outside the conference room where the test would be administered. Many traded stories about how many times they'd made it to this point in the process before.

Then the conference room doors swung open and everyone began to filter in. Once inside, I waved to Speak, who would be running the show that day, and she smiled back a little too warmly and walked in my direction.

"I think you should take the test," she said. "For the experience of it."

I told her I disagreed.

As the podium-dwellers of tomorrow sidled in, arranging themselves at long tables in front of sheets of paper scored with fifty empty slots, Speak shook her head. "You're going to take the test," she said.

While I might not have quiz-show smarts, I like to think I can at least identify a lost cause. I asked Speak if she would auto-flunk me to spare me the humiliation. "If you do well," she said, turning to the room of eager test-takers, "you'll get a chance on the show like everyone else."

Oh no. *Oh no.* I gulped and went to take a seat with everyone else.

Yours truly notwithstanding, the mood in the room quickly turned jovial. An AP Calc exam this is not: *Jeopardy!* auditions are fun, even raucous, by design. This is thanks to the intensely charismatic contestant coordinators, whose core job responsibilities can be thought of as: (1) Locate four-hundred-odd clever strangers to fill out the show every year, and (2) Make sure those clever strangers are actually enjoyable to watch on TV, which, generally speaking, happy people are, and people sweating bullets and wondering if they might throw up emphatically are not. Which is to say that the people in the *Jeopardy!* contestant department have advanced degrees in charming and soothing very nervous geeks, on both tape days and any other.

On this day, senior coordinator Corina Nusu led the room through the orientation, a snappy routine that both covered the basics—fifty questions at eight-second intervals, no "what is..." necessary, do *not* say the answers out loud—and somehow resulted in her goading the room into a live rendition of "Sweet Caroline."

(Nusu's powers of persuasion are not to be doubted. While Nusu was miking up contestant Michael Pascuzzi for a 2018 episode, Pascuzzi mentioned that his longtime girlfriend was sitting in the studio waiting to watch him play. Nusu offhandedly asked if he was going to "put a ring on it." "Should I do it now?" she remembers him asking. Minutes later, Nusu watched as Alex Trebek—who was given a heads-up about what was about to happen—ceded the Q&A floor to Pascuzzi, who asked Maria Shafer "if she would make [him] a winner today and marry" him. They wed the following year; Trebek sent a note wishing them "many years of happiness.")

"Who here likes 'Before & After'?" Nusu asked the room of the infamous, recurring wordplay category ported over from *Wheel of Fortune*. When a few people meekly murmured that they did, she shouted, "Liars!" She ran us through a few sample clues, and dread filled me as hands shot up over and over while I was still working them out.

After one, Nusu squinted into the crowd. "Hm," she said, considering which of the candidates to call on. "H-Bomb!"

Harvey Silikovitz, or, as he is known in trivia circles, H-Bomb, nailed it, and Nusu cheered.

For H-Bomb, getting on *Jeopardy!* has become something like a calling in life. In 2001, a friend who made it onto the show first encouraged him to try out. He did, scoring his first audition that year. As in this attempt in Las Vegas, he was required to take a fifty-question test upon his arrival; he failed and was sent home. Three years later, he auditioned again, and this time—with some concerted studying in the interim—he passed. But he never got called to go on, so he auditioned again the following year, and again nothing came of it.

In the years after that, H-Bomb, now fifty and a practicing attorney in New York City, devoted himself to *Jeopardy!*, trying out each and every time he had the chance. Counting the first failed test, Las Vegas marked his ninth audition, and a particularly bittersweet one, because it shouldn't have happened at all.

In March 2019, H-Bomb finally made it. Speak herself called him to deliver the happy news: After audition no. 8 in mid-2017, there was finally a spot for him on the show a few weeks hence, and all he had to do was call back, confirm, and book his flight to LA.

Only H-Bomb didn't get the message. Somehow, five weeks went by before he finally heard Speak's voicemail, but by the time he called back, taping for Season 35 had already wrapped. But the producers couldn't just slot him in for Season 36: By the time it was scheduled to start taping that summer, too much time would have elapsed since the 2017 audition—players only stay in the active pool for eighteen months after their audition—and H-Bomb's eligibility would be over.

So here he was once again. The whole time he was in Las Vegas, H-Bomb says, he was optimizing for his time in front of the producers. He blew off an earlier event for fear the hotel's climate-control chill would exacerbate a cough. He stayed in the night before. He meditated. Over the years, he's become a favorite presence at auditions; at her panel, Speak went so far as to call him out by name from the stage. "You've tried out how many times, Harvey?" she asked, and he told her. She remembered him. That had to be a good sign.

And now, suddenly, it was time. Kimberlin, H-Bomb, and I—plus sixty-seven other contenders—initialed our forms: I HAVE NEVER APPEARED ON ANY VERSION OF *JEOPARDY!* HOSTED BY ALEX TREBEK, we swore, using the *Jeopardy!*-branded clicker pens handed out to each of us, which the coordinators swore were just like the buzzers on the show.

Then a giant recording of Trebek filled a screen at the front of the room. "Although I can't be there in person," the host said, "I'd like to thank all of you for taking time to audition for our show."

By the sound of it, more than a few people were clicking their new pens for good luck.

CONTESTANT SKULDUGGERY

One of the most sacred rules of *Jeopardy!* is that once you've competed on the show, you can never do so again. There are only two ways for a player to return to *Jeopardy!*: an invitation to a reunion competition like the Tournament of Champions or else a rare mulligan granted due to a questioning misfire, as was the case for eventual seven-time champ Ryan Fenster. Fenster was brought back after his fifth-game loss when a *Jeopardy!* staffer belatedly found that his answer of "the Great Schism" was an acceptable alternative to "the Western Schism." As a result, Fenster is one of the few contestants to have taken home both the $1,000 third-place prize and—five months later—the $2,000 second-place prize. Plus, oh, $156,497 of winnings, and, having had the chance to reach the fifth win that guaranteed an invitation, another $5,000 from the Tournament of Champions.

But the rules haven't always been followed.

Enter Jeff Kirby. In the fall of 2009, Kirby, billed as "a math and science teacher from Santa Maria, California," appeared on *Jeopardy!*, where he came in third against Emma Span and reigning champion Terry Linwood. It was a good game, with Kirby and Linwood repeatedly swapping for the lead, which eventually went to Linwood after Kirby bet all but $300 on Final Jeopardy! and was wrong. A one-and-done is still plenty to be excited about, and so, as many contestants do, Kirby sat for an interview with his local newspaper to mark the occasion, telling the *Santa Maria Times* about his nerves and the on-set strangeness of, he said, "having makeup put on for the first time."

What he failed to mention was that he'd already been through the whole process a decade earlier.

Within a day of the 2009 episode airing, eagle-eyed viewers discovered Kirby's history. In 1999, Kirby—then billed as "an elementary school teacher from Santa Maria, California"—first played on the show, wearing what certainly looked to be the exact same red-and-white tie that he would wear in his second appearance. Just as he would in 2009, he finished in third place, and almost certainly had his face powdered on both occasions.

The show's producers were less than pleased by the revelation. "He did not disclose that he had previously been on *Jeopardy!*," the show declared in a statement, noting that if Kirby had, he would of course have been ineligible to compete. Kirby's $1,000 consolation prize—his second one, that is—was revoked.

Then there's the case of Barbara Lowe. In 1986, Lowe turned up on *Jeopardy!*, where she won five games and rankled viewers, not to mention *Jeopardy!* staff. During one episode, she openly challenged Trebek over the veracity of an answer. After pronouncing the names of the murderous University of Chicago students "Leopold and *Leeb*" and getting marked incorrect by Trebek, she scolded the host, insisting that *Leeb* was the correct German pronunciation of Loeb. He gave it to her.

Lowe walked away with roughly $50,000 and, given her five wins, a berth in the upcoming Tournament of Champions. Then the show was alerted to her duplicity: She had apparently been competing on a number of game shows under aliases. These appearances exceeded what was permitted under *Jeopardy!*'s policies—a fact she likely knew, given that her application failed to mention them—and the show decided to withhold her winnings. As Trebek recalled later to a reporter, "She had been on seven or eight other game shows under four other identities and Social Security numbers."

Lowe sued. In the end, the show settled, and did not invite her back for the 1986 Tournament of Champions. The player she beat in her first game, Lionel Goldbart, *was* invited, despite Lowe ending his streak at four victories. In the tournament, Goldbart achieved infamy when, at the very end of his semifinals match, he went all in on a Daily Double and then forgot to phrase his answer in the form of a question. "Oh, Lionel," said Trebek.

Goldbart, who came back for two more tournaments in the 1990s, was not your typical *Jeopardy!* contestant. His 2010 obituary in the *South Florida Sun Sentinel* described him as "an unrepentant speed freak" who "traveled in the same Greenwich Village circles as Jack Kerouac and Allen Ginsberg," and noted that $2,000 of his *Jeopardy!* winnings went to a friend "to install a urinal in her natural-foods restaurant."

As for Lowe: *Jeopardy!* suppressed reruns of her episodes, making them some of the few that have so far evaded the diligent episode catalogers at the J! Archive. In 2020, a contributor's discovery of a short, grainy clip that showed Lowe celebrating her second victory was cause for celebration—not to mention an update of the database.

It used to be even harder to get on *Jeopardy!*, at least from a logistical standpoint. For many years, auditions were held twice a day in the studio audience. Those who couldn't make it to LA instead had to catch up with a mobile testing center called the Brain Bus—that's right, the *Brain Bus*. The vinyl-wrapped Winnebago roved the country, stopping at choice libraries and malls where prospective contestants could take a ten-question preliminary test and, if they did well enough, come back the following day for an audition.

The Brain Bus's arrival was not exactly the circus pulling into town, but for a certain sort of cerebral suburbanite, it might as well have been. Passersby and pilgrims alike were invited to play a "just-for-fun" version of *Jeopardy!*, complete with authentic signaling devices. The bus often carried with it members of the Clue Crew, who doled out swag and autographs.

For the inaugural College Championship in 1989, candidates were recruited in a tent set up on the sand in Daytona Beach, Florida, during spring break. That year's champion, Tom Cubbage—who also won the subsequent Tournament of Champions and has been back for three additional reunion tournaments—recalled that at the time he "was just walking down the beach and saw a banner that said they were doing *Jeopardy!* tryouts."

Before the Brain Bus, things were even more dire. Would-be players of old had to resort to mailing in postcards ahead of regional auditions. The odds weren't great: Before the show's first recruiting visit to New York City, it received a baffling twenty-two thousand cards for four hundred total interview slots—not a few of them repeat entries from hopefuls trying to improve their chances. (Eventual 1996 Tournament of Champions winner Michael Dupée sent 319 cards before his own audition, postmarked with $60 worth of stamps.) When a visit to Washington, DC, was announced in 1987, the local affiliate, WJLA-TV, got thirty thousand cards.

The show insisted that candidates would be selected at random, which did little to deter senders from making their case by hand. In 2018, photographer Sofie Mathiassen discovered a cache of applicant postcards from the 1990s at an antiques store in Akron, Ohio. Her findings—postmarked, so apparently delivered, though no one at the store could explain how they ended up in Ohio—offer a portrait of eagerness bordering on desperation.

"Dear *Jeopardy!*," wrote one candidate, "I am a 38-year-old teacher (vastly underpaid) who would like to be on your show. I've been watching for about 15 years." "I am such a fan of *Jeopardy!*," wrote another, "I drive everyone I know at work, my friends, and family absolutely *Jeopardy!* crazy! I know I will do great and make a presence on the show! PICK ME. PICK ME. PICK ME!"

So rejoice, aspiring contestants of the twenty-first century—you have it easier. Which is not, unfortunately, the same thing as *easy*.

The total number of slots on *Jeopardy!* in any given year is static. In a season with no special tournaments taking the place of normal games, there are 230 new episodes of regular *Jeopardy!* gameplay. Assuming that there were no three-way ties for zero, that means that just 460 players, plus the season debut's returning champion, would get a spot on the show. Because tournaments frequently do get in the way, the real number of openings is usually even smaller.

TOURNAMENTS ON *JEOPARDY!*

Further limiting the openings on *Jeopardy!* are the show's regular tournaments. Most modern seasons feature a Teen Tournament, College Championship, and Teachers Tournament, all featuring first-time *Jeopardy!* contestants. While the teen and college contests have their own dedicated application pathway—parents of adolescent Jeopardians receive the ominous message in their inbox: "Your child wants to become a contestant on *Jeopardy!*"—the Teachers Tournament pulls from the regular *Jeopardy!* contestant pool: a sign of just how many educators try out for the show.

The winners of the two adult contests are given berths in the show's cornerstore reunion competition: the Tournament of Champions, in which fifteen players face off for a $250,000 grand prize.

Even better, perhaps, than that grand prize? An invitation to more reunion tournaments. The top finishers in the Tournament of Champions are often tapped for future contests. Recent years have featured the All-Star Games and the Greatest of All Time tournament; a betting woman might look forward to what the show has in store in 2024, the revival's fortieth-anniversary season. Indeed, the success of the GOAT tournament, which aired on

ABC, convinced the powers that be that the *Jeopardy!* public could embrace new formats. In 2021, Mayim Bialik hosted the first-ever college professor tournament.

Pour one out for the *Jeopardy!* Seniors Tournament, which has not been held since 1995, and Kids Week, which has not been seen since 2014. According to a cache of emails published that year after Sony was hacked in an attack later attributed to the government of North Korea, the preceding Kids Week had been something of a debacle after a parent took issue with Trebek's brusqueness toward her child. When producers asked Trebek to retape a segment, the incensed host threatened to leave the show. "If I'm making mistakes and saying things you don't like," he dictated in a message to the show's top producers, "maybe it's time for me to move on."

Given the choice between the host and Kids Week—well, you can draw your own conclusion.

The number of test-takers each year, on the other hand, keeps growing. You might recall that more than a hundred and twenty-five thousand people take the test in a normal year; when Ken Jennings applied in 2003, he faced a pool of just ("just") thirty thousand. In 2020, the show introduced the Anytime Test, transforming what had been an online exam offered just once a year into one awaiting anyone who might be interested year-round. In just the first three months of the

Anytime Test, nearly 100,000 hopefuls took it, according to *Jeopardy!* You can try your luck at getting on *Jeopardy!* from your couch these days, but the problem is that everyone else can, too.

Before she inducted me into the ranks of the test-takers, Speak sat down with me to explain what goes into the process of whittling down the applicant pool. Even knowing that she is a professional charmer is little defense against her warmth: "Oh, I *love* your shirt!" she gushes before declaring that she might steal it from me, and I am in that moment convinced that my shirt—an utterly bland button-down purchased the day before mostly for the sake of adding a layer ahead of some long days indoors—is the finest shirt in all the land.

"People say, 'I don't want to take the test, I know I won't pass the test,'" says Speak. "And the best advice that I have is: 'Let the test tell you.'"

The big surprise for many applicants is that *Jeopardy!* isn't *just* looking for the smartest possible contestants. That is, yes, the single most important piece of it, hence the test. But the criteria extend well beyond smarts. *Jeopardy!* is, first and foremost, a TV show, and the producers are trying to put together a program that is cerebral *and* entertaining, and whose players look something like the audience at home, plus or minus a couple of advanced degrees.

So while the contestant pool is not necessarily the most diverse place—Speak tells me, for one, that roughly 75 percent of the people who take the contestant test in any given year are men, a skew that's also reflected in much of the trivia world at large—the program tries to do better. Casting on *Jeopardy!* looks for diversity in categories obvious and less so: gender, ethnicity, age (the audience hews decidedly more silver than the typical contestant), home state, *part* of the home state, even profession. "For a while," says Speak, "bartenders were super hot."

Austin Rogers, a twelve-time champion in 2017 and perhaps the best-known beneficiary of the bartender trend, has said that he suspects that applying as a bartender—the job he took on after being laid off by an ad agency—probably helped. "I still would have had the same energy," he told a reporter after his run concluded, "but I don't think I would have resonated if I was Rogers the digital ad guy, or Rogers the corporate events planner."

In short: Having a good tagline doesn't hurt.

The producers want people who will make good TV— some small-screen *je ne sais quoi* that might give the folks on the couch someone to root for. (Yes, this means the brittle geniuses you've been watching expound on their love of socks and boiled potatoes night after night actually won their respective personality contests. In the early years of the original version of *Jeopardy!*, NBC complained that the show's contestants "looked like Marxist radicals," Merv Griffin wrote in his 1980 autobiography, *Merv*. But "we weren't running a beauty contest," he continued. "I explained we wanted game-players.")

"It's really hard to describe what that element is going to be that will make them spark our interest and sing on the show," Speak says. "Sometimes it's somebody who plays so brilliantly you just can't believe it. Sometimes it's somebody who's having so much fun with it, and still doing well. Basically, there's got to be something about how they play that makes you want to watch them play."

Put differently: While it's *possible* that a very good but

otherwise boring trivia player might get on the show, academic skill alone is probably not enough. Nobody was clamoring for Watson—the IBM computer that defeated Jennings and Rutter in a two-game showdown in 2011—to get its own spinoff.

"There are some people who just want to play so seriously and they don't want to have any fun," says Speak. "And I get that sometimes the game is serious but, you know, try to have a little bit of fun with us."

Easier said than done.

In the interim between the *Jeopardy!* test and the auditions, I found myself suddenly in the same spirals of anxiety I'd so casually been asking interview subjects about for weeks.

Did I have any interesting personal stories—any at all? Would Trebek, in some theoretical future, laugh when I told him that MC Hammer blocked me on Twitter after I wrote a story he didn't like, or would that take too long to explain? Or, worse, would he have a follow-up question? Perhaps I should just play it safe and talk about how I got engaged. Or—maybe that I have a cat? And anyway, wouldn't I just embarrass myself in the practice game?

Mercifully, if not unpredictably, I flunked the test. As if in a high school movie with assignments for the big play, sheets went up outside the conference room showing that of the seventy people who took the morning's test, thirty-nine would be asked to participate in the afternoon portion. That is a significantly higher rate than the normal testing pool, perhaps speaking to the kind of person who books a trip to Las Vegas when they hear that *Jeopardy!* producers will be in town.

For the second half of the audition, which I would now

happily be back to simply observing, those who passed were split into two groups. As at normal auditions, the final task is a mock game, with contestant coordinators calling up players three by three to face off for a portion of a board with buzzers—real, honest-to-Merv buzzers—in hand. And as at normal auditions, the coordinators have exceedingly little interest in whether players get the answers right.

If the original question plaguing an audition attendee was *Am I smart enough to get on* Jeopardy!*?*, it is now something much more horrifying: *Am I charismatic enough to get on* Jeopardy!*?*

Three by three, would-be contestants were summoned to the front of the room, where Speak, Nusu, and assorted *Jeopardy!* staff waited. The process vaguely mimics what happens on the show: Players answer a few questions (or, more accurately, question a few answers), ringing in with a lectern-less system reminiscent of Schantz's simulator. Here, the contestant coordinators want to know: Can you have fun, or pretend to have fun semi-convincingly, or at least not actively seem to be not having fun, while playing high-stakes trivia on national TV? Can you mask the symptoms of palmoplantar hyperhidrosis well enough to hang on to your buzzer? Can you follow the instructions about where to stand, and hold back an eye roll when the twerp next to you rings in wrong on a no-doubter? Can you look even just very slightly less terrified than you currently are?

"You having any fun, Tim?" Speak shouts at one nervous newcomer. "Let's see that smile."

"Big voice!" calls Nusu.

"Look alive for us, Molly!"

"Don't lose your energy!"

"A little bit louder voice—*good*."

The terrible part comes after the questions, as the coordinators turn to each player one by one as everyone watches: *So, Bob, tell me about yourself.*

For those who've already been to this particular rodeo, this segment of the audition is often a source of obsession. If you've tried out for *Jeopardy!* before and didn't get the call to come on afterward, you never know for sure what went wrong. Maybe you didn't do as well on your in-person test as you thought you did. (But you compared notes with other people afterward and are certain you got a forty-eight out of fifty!) Maybe there just weren't enough slots on the show for strong candidates. (Come on—a *forty-eight!*) Or maybe—the most dreadful option of all and therefore the one most tempting to dwell on, month after month, *Jeopardy!* episode after *Jeopardy!* episode—you flunked the personality portion of the test. (As they say: WECIB? *What else could it be?*)

At auditions, coordinators lead prospective contestants through the kinds of personal anecdotes that might pop up after the first commercial break: unusual hobbies, spousal meet-cutes, that time they went to Europe.

Many hopefuls prepare extensively for this interrogation, memorizing a collection of lightly quirky one-liners and modestly embellished truths about how they would spend their theoretical spoils. One told me days before the audition that he intended to talk about his nonexistent plans to build a catio (that's a patio for—you get it), but worried it wasn't interesting enough.

Others apparently didn't worry quite as much: A math teacher loves cats (this is, clearly, a cat person crowd); a pharmaceutical salesman is a fan of movies. One player reveals that shortly after arriving in Las Vegas, he came down with crippling stomach pain and went to see a doctor; his appendix was removed just twenty-four hours before the audition. "So if I'm a little slouchy..." he trailed off. He was given a round of applause and a *Jeopardy!* board game for his trouble, and one or two of those yet to interview looked vaguely jealous of his tale.

"The weirdest thing I ever heard was at a college audition," Speak tells the room. "A young man said he was going to buy a cave in which he could make goat cheese. He said nothing about a goat. He said nothing about equipment or lessons. All I heard was *it puts the lotion on its skin.*"

The coordinators make a point of trying to knock players off their talking points, buffeting them with cheerful small talk—*what do you do for a living? For fun? What did you say you're writing historical fiction about again?*—before they can finish their prepared remarks.

Some pass this test—a screenwriter from LA placidly offers up her favorite restaurants as if this is a perfectly normal chat and not a potentially life-altering exchange—following the line of conversation and perhaps even getting in the occasional joke. Others, especially those burned by past audition attempts, just want to get through their lines. Wooden recital is perhaps not the best response to a test of basic television readiness, but nerves are nerves.

Silikovitz—alias H-Bomb—did not seem particularly nervous, despite the fact that he found himself called up first. During his spin in front of the contestant coordinators, he launched into some impromptu karaoke—he's a collector of international karaoke destinations, having now sung on every continent but Antarctica—and belted out the lyrics to "La Bamba" to the coordinators' obvious delight; he tacked on what he called his "trademark H-Bomb leg kick" for good measure. Later, he told me he was sure he nailed it: "It was the best I've ever felt coming out of an audition," he said.

Jeopardy! has long been a singular goal in H-Bomb's life, but in recent months, it has loomed larger still. Shortly after Trivia Nationals, Silikovitz was diagnosed with Parkinson's disease. A few months later, he told me that after some initial physical therapy and lifestyle adjustments, even his neurologist had marveled at his improvement, and he had high hopes of slowing the disease's progression to a crawl.

"I feel very strongly that I don't want to be defined by this disease that I have," he said. And so he was carrying on with all the things he always has: travel (a trip to Cuba, and doubtless a Cuban karaoke bar, awaited), trivia (he had already registered for next summer's Trivia Nationals), and, yes, *Jeopardy!* Surely, having missed the call the previous spring, this ninth attempt would be the charm.

So far, one of his chief complaints has been that the time he now devotes to physical therapy eats away at hours he otherwise might devote to studying or buzzer practice. But H-Bomb was thriving in his recreational trivia league, and the reflexes in his buzzer hand were as sharp as ever (he times himself using a website popular with *Jeopardy!* trainees). He called the producers, in fact, to tell them about his diagnosis and his continuing certainty that he could compete with the best of 'em. Every night, he stands while he watches *Jeopardy!*, the better to be prepared for when he plays the real thing.

All he was waiting for, as ever, was the call.

For H-Bomb, there were a lot of reasons to go on *Jeopardy!*— and, therefore, a lot of reasons to shape his life around the possibility. "I'm not going to say that the chance to win a lot of money isn't one of them," he says.

But there is so much more. He's been trying to get on *Jeopardy!* for so long now—has become friends with so many people he considered *Jeopardy!* mentors. Every other week, he meets a group of fellow *Jeopardy!* hopefuls for a game of trivia at the Hell's Kitchen pub where bartender Austin Rogers writes the questions himself.

"My trivia team never wins at his pub quiz, partly because we're spectacularly bad at the audio rounds," says Silikovitz. "But we frequently win the last round, which he calls 'Random Shit You Should Know,' which results in us winning free shots."

Once, after an audition, a fellow applicant told Silikovitz that when he had to talk to the producers immediately after him, he felt like the guy who followed the Beatles on *The Ed Sullivan Show*. But H-Bomb's phone never rang, and late in Season 36, he was still waiting to hear back from *Jeopardy!* But he wasn't sweating it. "One thing I am is very persistent," he says.

As auditions wrapped in Las Vegas, coordinators sent the players on their way. All names, they were told, had been entered into the *Jeopardy!* contestant pool, which means they could be summoned at any point in the next eighteen months. And that's that. They'll call, maybe. Keep the pen! It's great for buzzer practice! Bye now!

And now they wait.

CHAPTER THREE

AND NOW, HERE IS THE HOST OF *JEOPARDY!*, ALEX TREBEK

A mong the stranger things about Alex Trebek is that he had spent nearly half his life living in three simultaneous time lines.

Time line one: the present, in which he, like the rest of us, went to work, did his job, and came home.

Time line two: two months in the future, filming episodes where he warmly wished his audience greetings for whatever season or holiday would be in full swing when the episode finally airs. (A 1998 contestant, Bob Harris, once recalled the shock of Trebek appearing onstage during his first game dressed as the Statue of Liberty, eventually realizing that although they were taping in mid-September, the episode would air on Halloween.)

And time line three: the past, keeping careful track of whichever months-old taping was just reaching the airwaves on any given day, so that he could tell you in cheerful present tense, for example, about the remarkable run of then-rampaging eight-time champ Karen Farrell—despite the fact that he'd actually witnessed Farrell's streak, and eventual loss, weeks earlier.

It would get any diarist tied up, but Trebek, at any rate, had some practice. Beginning in 1984, when he became the host of *Jeopardy!*, *today* was a flexible term.

"I was told by a producer many, many years ago," Trebek told the *Today* show in 2016, "'Alex, this is a precarious business, and if somebody makes a job offer—take it.'"

⟵

Off-camera, Trebek was decidedly more casual—funnier, sharper, more self-deprecating—than he was on it. Gone was the prickly schoolteacher. In his place instead appeared someone seemingly relaxed and grandfatherly, even occasionally kooky—the kind of person who, whenever the game board malfunctioned in *Jeopardy!*'s earliest years, would slip off a shoe during the resulting delay and hurl it in the board's direction in mock-rage, to the delight of those in the studio.

"Julia?" Trebek calls this morning to Julia Collins from the *Jeopardy!* audience, where he sits wearing glasses and a USO button-down—a memento from one of his many overseas entertainment tours—as he flips through the day's material.

He had glanced up at Collins, at the time the owner of the second-longest winning streak in *Jeopardy!* history, who had backed away from the player lecterns during a pause in rehearsals and was swaying in place, arms wrapped around herself. "Are you freezing again?"

Trebek and I first met in early 2019, as the show filmed its first-ever (and likely last-ever) team tournament, the All-Star Games, which featured eighteen of the show's most notable contestants from years past. The tournament was a decidedly strange project for *Jeopardy!*, if only because it was something totally new. All week long, production staff hurried around Stage 10, working out unfamiliar blocking and angles.

Collins says she's fine, but Trebek won't be rebuffed. "If you need your jacket just put it on," he shouts, "'cause it's cold in here."

David Letterman was said to keep the studio at the Ed Sullivan Theater at an uncomfortable fifty-five degrees year-round, a policy that invited a number of conspiracy theories, some more plausible than others. He did it to avoid breaking a sweat or to keep his audience from falling asleep, maybe, or else to protest the network's refusal to install more efficient LED lighting. My favorite: Following a thermostat experiment he allegedly conducted in the 1980s, he came to believe that that was the temperature at which his jokes landed best.

In any case, the *Jeopardy!* soundstage is kept to a Minneapolis-in-March cool. "It's got some weird kind of chilled TV odor in here," jokes Ken Jennings, another one of the All-Stars, "that when I get a glimpse or whiff of it somewhere else, it always makes me have a flashback. I feel like it makes me play better to have that kind of *Jeopardy!* smell." Collins put on a coat.

The day before taping was set to begin, Trebek opted to

do his usual morning review of the material out in the open—the better to get a sense of the tournament's flow, perhaps, or simply because these players are the ones the host has come to know best. In the case of Jennings and Brad Rutter, they were coming up on two full decades of working together, in a manner of speaking.

Audiences at first were wary of Trebek. His affable predecessor, Art Fleming, had been popular during the original *Jeopardy!*'s initial eleven-year run, from 1964 to 1975. When the program returned a decade later with a new host, viewers complained that the new show was easier, its questions too simple; a *Los Angeles Times* critic declared the new host "unctuous," the show "a shadow of what [viewers] once knew." If it improved somewhat, it was only because of the original's influence: "I can only hope it was Fleming who gave Trebek his much-needed dignity transplant," the critic concluded. So divisive was Trebek that in 1990, *Washington Post* columnist Tony Kornheiser imagined the US Census asking citizens "Do you prefer Art Fleming to Alex Trebek?" as a way of determining "our true feelings." (Kornheiser also suggested the curiously still-relevant "Should Pete Rose make the Hall of Fame?")

Trebek didn't set out to be a game-show lifer: In 1986, he told a reporter that he originally saw hosting as "merely an avenue through which I could break into show business."

By the time *Jeopardy!* came around, Trebek was something of an old hand in television, which he had by then spent two decades working in. He had come to Hollywood at age thirty-three from his native Canada, where he had been a news broadcaster for the CBC. Trebek's rise had been swift at the national broadcaster, the result of what he long considered a series of lucky breaks. He got his first full-time job there when he, still a student at the University of Ottawa, offered to take undesirable hours and holiday shifts by coming in after his morning classes. Two years later, Trebek was promoted into the Toronto headquarters because, thanks to his French-Canadian mother, Lucille, he was the only member of the English staff who also spoke perfect French.

His career as a game-show host began in a suite at the Hilton in New York City. In Toronto, Trebek had hosted an afternoon talk show, on which fellow Canadian and future *Growing Pains* star Alan Thicke performed. Thicke decamped for Los Angeles, where he signed on to produce a new NBC game show called *The Wizard of Odds*. While searching for a host who could handle some ad-libbing, Thicke suggested Trebek, who flew to New York for a dry run, with an audience of passersby collected outside the Hilton.

The network apparently liked what it saw: Thicke called Trebek to offer him the job later that night, after Trebek had already flown back north to catch the last two periods of the night's hockey game. (His blood ran bleu, blanc, et rouge as a longtime Montreal Canadiens fan.) His thick brown mustache and 1970s halo of maybe-perm—the CBC used to insist on straightening it—had apparently sealed the deal: He was, he said, the first game-show host with a mustache since Groucho Marx. The pilot was picked up, and so Trebek resigned from the CBC and joined Thicke in California.

But *The Wizard of Odds*, whose opening posited such enigmas as "What will the average man reveal when he unbuttons his shirt?" and "What are the odds that you kiss and tell more than the average girl, Lavonne?" was not to last; it was canceled in 1974 after a single season, on the very day that Trebek signed the final papers to buy his first house in LA.

He had a new gig by the start of the following week: *High Rollers*, which featured oversize dice and a little more stability: Trebek stayed put for four and a half years, with a stint hosting a neon-infused third game show, *Double Dare*, in the middle. (Not to be confused with the Nickelodeon game show that appeared a decade later under the same name. Trebek's version, for better or worse, did not feature a Sundae Slide or tickets to Space Camp.)

"I deserve it," he said to rapturous applause from a *Double Dare* studio audience in one episode, "but we must go on."

But stability, alas, isn't quite what showbiz is known for. *High Rollers* was canceled in 1980, and then came a procession of other hosting gigs, among them *Battlestars* ("In what key do the majority of American car horns beep in?" he asked a flustered Debbie Reynolds) and *Malcolm* (a dreadful unsold 1983 pilot, in which Trebek co-hosted with a cartoon).

Back in early 1981, he'd landed a gig with a Canadian game show called *Pitfall* and filmed 26 weeks of programming. By 1982, however, the show's packager, Catalena Productions, had gone bankrupt, and Trebek's check bounced. Decades later, the host still kept the bounced check framed on a wall in his home.

He had been out of work for nearly a year when *Jeopardy!* came along. His first job with Merv Griffin Enterprises was actually at *Wheel of Fortune*: When Chuck Woolery, who hosted *Wheel* from 1975 to 1981, was hospitalized, Trebek was asked to guest-host in his place for several episodes. After Griffin, who was looking to pair a *Jeopardy!* revival with *Wheel* in syndication, approached Trebek, he demanded producer duties (and, ahem, salary) alongside the hosting gig. With no particular hopes for this new game-show foray to endure, Griffin and syndicator King World agreed.

Even after he began hosting *Jeopardy!*, Trebek occasionally dabbled in other shows on the side, including a run with *Classic Concentration* and the *Pillsbury Bake-Off*. In 1991, he briefly hosted *To Tell the Truth*, whose format had a trio of challengers claim to be the same real-life person before submitting to questions from a panel whose members voted on who they thought was the genuine article. Trebek's *Truth* spin occasionally veered into the bizarre, such as in an episode featuring actress Sharon Tate's mother, Doris, who had become a victim's rights advocate following her daugher's notorious death.

"For years after my pregnant daughter and six others were murdered by the Manson family," Trebek solemnly read on the real Doris's behalf, "I was immobilized by grief." (The situation only got stranger as panelists began peppering Tate and the "impostor" challengers with questions. "Number three," asked one panelist, "are there a *lot* of children who get murdered?" Another inquired—of one of the false Dorises, no less—if she went to therapy.)

Trebek was forty-four when the *Jeopardy!* revival debuted, and he wasn't *not* meant as eye candy. A story in the *Los Angeles Times* early in his *Jeopardy!* tenure noted that he, with his signature mustache, "could be an unusually handsome professor" and was "more than just another pretty suit" before making mention of the—pardon me while I loosen my necktie—"throbbing electronic *Jeopardy!* set."

People ran a breathless story on the then-single host under the headline "Sorry, Girls, Mom Keeps House for *Jeopardy!* Host Alex Trebek," in reference to the fact that Lucille shared his Hollywood Hills mansion-slash-bachelor-pad. Trebek joked about asking out *Wheel of Fortune* hostess Vanna White, noting that she was quite intelligent: "She always turns me down," he said.

In the mid-'80s, *Jeopardy!* ran a series of ads showcasing the host as a Bond-esque man of mystery, rescuing various scantily clad damsels in distress. "We risked everything for these questions," gasped one just-liberated woman as a tuxedo-clad Trebek rushed her past her captors' gunfire; "That's why we call it *Jeopardy!*" the host replied. "*Jeopardy!* is my life," he cooed to a different woman, who was wrapped in a bathrobe after being fished out of the sea by Trebek. Said he: "It's the *second* most exciting game I know." Hubba hubba.

When Trebek ditched his soup strainer in 1997, it was mourned in *People* as one might an actual person: "Host Alex Trebek, 59, has shaved off his mustache, 20." The magazine pulled no punches—the headline was "Alex Trebek: Naked."

At his wedding to Jean Currivan in 1990, private security ejected no fewer than five tabloid reporters from the nuptials, who could be overheard gabbing about Jean's dress to editors from a nearby pay phone booth. For his vows, Trebek responded, "The answer is...yes."

They learned they were expecting their first child, Matthew, just three weeks after the ceremony. When Matthew was a baby, Trebek joked that he and Jean could hear him over the monitor in the morning humming the *Jeopardy!* theme song. Fitting enough, given it was written for Griffin's own infant son.

THE CLUE CREW

When the Clue Crew was first introduced in 2001, Alex Trebek insisted that he was scared for his job. "I hope they're not too good," he told *Entertainment Weekly*, "because then somebody will look at them and say, 'Geez, we ought to think about replacing Trebek.'"

The announcement that the venerable game show was looking to hire a quartet of correspondents to travel the globe in search of *Jeopardy!* clues had been an occasion for low-grade trivia mania. Some five thousand applications poured in, with would-be Clue Crew members juggling oranges, reciting Dr. Seuss poetry, and putting on their best faux-Trebek.

In the years since, segments have taken the Clue Crew to all seven continents and nearly fifty countries, with locales like Easter Island, Petra, Machu Picchu, Churchill Downs, the Tsukiji fish market, and the Galápagos Islands (twice with Trebek in tow). Two members of the original team remain with the show: Sarah Whitcomb Foss and Jimmy McGuire. It's not all exotic adventure, as Foss demonstrated for a clue in the 2001 category "'Bel'lissimo!" "Unfortunately," she said just before hurling herself facedown into a pool, "it's what I'm about to do here." (That would be a belly flop: "You couldn't pay me enough to do that!" Trebek exclaimed to players during the game.)

For *Jeopardy!*, the Clue Crew isn't just a sunny accompaniment to the show's long-standing video clues. Its members have long lent a hand at auditions and during practice games; in 2021, McGuire became the show's stage manager following the retirement of John Lauderdale, while Foss often filled in as the announcer. Original member Sofia Dickens (née Lidskog) said she received an assortment of fan mail during her years on the Clue Crew—many of them teenage boys asking her to prom.

On-destination clues are banked months or years in advance, such that McGuire says he doesn't always remember filming them by the time they air. "You can't just show up at the Vatican and shoot," says Brett Schneider, who led the Clue Crew as *Jeopardy!*'s segment director. "My friends think I just run around filling up my passport with stamps," jokes Schneider, who says that China and Hong Kong are in his sights. "And it's actually a lot of phone calls, faxing, and email in advance."

The trips have not always gone as planned. Once, while preparing for a shoot atop a glacier in Alaska, the pilot warned the group to look out for moulins—deep fissures in the ice, which, says Schneider, "you can fall through and never be seen again." The helicopter touched down on the glacier, and the Clue Crew, cameraperson, audio supervisor, et al., piled out to begin the shoot.

"And next thing I knew, our helicopter pilot, who looked about fifteen, was shouting, 'Back in! Back in!' The helicopter was starting to slide down the glacier."

Planning segments is easy enough in the US, where *Jeopardy!* and Trebek are household names and it's rarely difficult convincing an organization, be it the National Museum of African American History and Culture or *The Harvard Lampoon*, of the show's reach. That's not always the case outside the States, says Schneider. "When I shoot abroad, it's kind of tough explaining what the show is to Lithuanians."

As Trebek walks into his dressing room, he spots my phone on the table in front of his couch. It's there as a backup recording, just in case my actual recorder alongside it decides to eat our interview.

"You're recording on both?" he asks, folding himself onto the couch. Yes, I tell him, just in ca—

He leans eagerly over the phone. "Can you hear me now?" he asks more loudly, knocking furiously on the table. "Can you hear me?"

He turns back to me and grins. "I just blew your machines right off," he says.

Trebek has changed—he's ditched the button-down and is now nearly stage-ready: hair and makeup done, dressed in suit pants and shirt and tie, though no jacket. But he's tired. He's fighting a bad cold—not to point any fingers, but your reporter came down with her own bad cold a few days later—and thought at one point he might even lose his voice.

It's not helping that this week is filled, as so few *Jeopardy!* weeks are, with *new*: new introductions, new cues, new gaps in the game. Later, I'll watch the tournament tape from the audience alongside a longtime studio hand, who seems genuinely shocked on the handful of occasions that Trebek misspeaks or accidentally skips something that he has to go back and redo—usually, those kinds of things are so rare that he struggles to think of ever seeing more than one or two in a tape day.

But this tournament has Trebek grumbling. By the week's end, the host will have had his fill of the stopping and starting, the subbing in of teammates and pausing so they can talk strategy offstage, and tells anyone who will hear it: He is never doing another All-Star Games. He's not the only one—a contestant tells me that he overheard the show's stage manager, John Lauderdale, who is also the stage manager at *Wheel of Fortune*, griping to Harry Friedman: "This is annoying as hell, man." The existing *Jeopardy!* model works perfectly well, thank you very much.

Over thirty-six years, with five suit changes two days a week, it is entirely possible that Trebek has worn more suits than anyone else in history. While we speak, I catch a glimpse of a rack in the adjoining closet that's lined with dozens of neat black and navy blazers. The ties can't be far behind: He claims to have never thrown any away, though some have been disbursed in *Jeopardy!* giveaways, and boasts that he has bolo ties and even dreaded "wide ties" at home. "I have *more* than 250," Trebek will say later, a little like it might be a threat, or at least something Jean is extremely aware of.

"I have suits that are older than half the members of our staff," he says. "Nothing gets thrown away."

On game shows, it was long traditional for the host of the program to also be introduced as the star. On *Jeopardy!*'s first-ever episode with Fleming in 1964, he was indeed introduced as such—and why not, given he's the one who was there week after week, season after season. So was Trebek on many of the shows he did before *Jeopardy!*: He was "the star of *M'ama Non M'ama*," a dismal reboot of an Italian dating show, and, on *The $128,000 Question* (a revival of its *$64,000* predecessor), "the host and star of our show." But when he took over the *Jeopardy!* reboot in 1984, he was adamant: He was the host. The *contestants* were the stars, and Johnny Gilbert introduced him accordingly from that point on.

But it's hard to deny the reality that nearly forty years at the center of one of American television's most popular programs gave him some star power. When school and tour groups and game-show obsessives would line up outside for the chance to spend a couple of hours inside the *Jeopardy!* studio, they were as interested, maybe more interested, in seeing the host as they were in seeing all those shiny blue set pieces. So great was the demand that the show has put out, alongside an enormous glass case with the dozens of gleaming Emmys racked up by *Jeopardy!* over the years (it had won 41 by the start of Season 38), a cardboard cutout of Trebek in the lobby for people to take pictures with. And did they ever.

"It takes a little while to get to like somebody," Trebek says of television, leaning back into the couch cushions.

He's talking about contestants—audiences took a while to warm up to Austin Rogers, he says, but when they settled into his rhythm, accepted that he was going to play a kookier game than they were used to, they started rooting for him. But the same might apply to Trebek, too.

"*Jeopardy!* has become so much a part of Americana and so much a part of the daily life of American TV viewers," he says, "that they feel comfortable with us." Fair enough— Trebek himself became an American citizen in 1997 and received a jury duty summons all of two weeks later, so he'd know as well as anyone, perhaps—but it raises the question: Is the audience adjusting to the person on television, or is the person on television adjusting to the audience?

HOW MUCH MONEY DID IT TAKE TO IMPRESS ALEX TREBEK?

Game shows give away money. Sure, yes, there's the game part, but the main thing that happens in your average half-hour studio contest is somebody wins some dough. So how do hosts crown their victors?

On *Wheel of Fortune*, Pat Sajak rarely diverges from chivalrous pride in his charges' victories: Good work; bang-up job; enjoy your convertible; keep your ears clean; ta-ta.

Steve Harvey, host of *Family Feud*, is uniformly

joyful and a little bit scattered. By the time someone wins, he's already had the chance to do what his viewers are really there to see: let contestants walk themselves into a trap of overexuberance or accidental revelation, allowing Harvey to lean back and sputter at the camera in pantomime disbelief.

Alex Trebek's prickliness, on the other hand, as so reliable that his rare exuberances took on mythic proportions. In 2019, the writer and designer Rex Sorgatz went so far as to create an online "Trebek Affirmation Soundboard," a clickable Double Jeopardy! board on which each selected clue reveals an upbeat Trebek quip from an episode. "It's a common mistake; we all make it," he says soothingly for $1,600; at $2,000, "You got it, yes! That was a tough one." The soundboard, which Sorgatz captioned "for those distressing moments in life when you could use an audible nudge of encouragement," swiftly went viral.

Part of the trouble in winning Trebek's approval, perhaps, is that the ceiling on *Jeopardy!* is high. It is possible, in theory, to top $500,000 in a single episode, though this is not a terribly likely outcome at this particular point on the space-time continuum. The single-game record—$131,127— was set by James Holzhauer in 2019 and is itself a baffling feat.

There's also the fact that *Jeopardy!* contestants,

unlike so many of their game-show peers, have the opportunity to come back to the stage, since the winner of each episode carries on to the next one; their winnings, in theory, are limitless. They have the chance to win it all, and boy, did Trebek want them to.

Even one of the show's most beloved champions, Ken Jennings, seemed to infuriate Trebek by not pushing his winnings higher. On three occasions, Jennings tied—but did not exceed—the then-record $52,000 total for one-day winnings set the year before.

Jennings acknowledged that the forbearance was a deliberate tribute to Brian Weikle, the previous record holder. "I didn't want to beat him by a dollar," Jennings explained on CBS's *The Early Show*, saying that Weikle had been a great player.

But Trebek openly egged him on to wager more. Jennings eventually appeased him, smashing the record with $75,000 in the Season 20 finale.

Because *Jeopardy!* is hard by design, and because each brainy *Jeopardy!* contestant is obligated to play against two other brainy *Jeopardy!* contestants, the vast majority of players don't quite break things open. During 2017–2018's Season 34, for example—a typical year for the show—the average winner took home $20,022, according to the J! Archive database. To be sure: That's a great deal of money to go home with in exchange for an afternoon of trivia, particularly given that prizes at local pub trivia nights are typically measured in pitchers of beer.

Trebek, however, did not seem to share this outlook. He wanted players to win, and wanted them to win big. If they didn't, the odds were good that they were going to hear about it.

In December 2016, for example, after four consecutive games in which winners failed to top $17,000, the host sounded a gloomy note: "In case you're joining us for the first time this week, I'll just say it's been a weird, weird week. Enough said."

By *weird* he meant "low-earning." Boring. *Disgraceful.* Best not to talk about it at all. Enough said.

Sometimes, though, he did talk about it: "$9,200 only for Sean yesterday," Trebek opened apologetically during another game, recounting the previous match's low earnings. Addressing his two new contestants, he told them, "I'll express the same thing I said yesterday: I hope we get a big payday today! It's up to you guys.

"Don't let me down!" Trebek added. You know, like all the other bozos who did let him down. Like that bozo, Sean, who was standing right there. Less than $10,000! Trebek offered him riches! He offered him glory! The whole world before him! And what did he do? He *let Trebek down.*

"It wasn't easy today, was it?" he asked a $10,800

winner. When three players entered Final Jeopardy! in an October 2019 game with the leader, eventual three-day champ Kevin Boettcher, at just $5,600, the host could not, or at least would not, contain his disappointment.

"I'm so glad this is not a Friday show, because I wouldn't want to end the week with a low-scoring final," he said.

Trebek, renderer of justice, did offer mercy to those he felt had earned it. When a champion he'd earlier mocked for her first-game total of $7,800 won her second game with a more respectable $21,200 in hand, Trebek seemed soothed. "Wow," he said. "What a way to end the week."

But sometimes there was no mercy to be found. In one game in January 2016, all three players managed to finish with $0.

His contestants laughed nervously, but Trebek remained stone-faced. Apparently done addressing the three losers—just a clinical diagnosis; *Jeopardy!* is a place where precision is rewarded—he turned to the audience. None of the contestants, he explained, would appear in the next game. "Sorry, folks," he said, gesturing at the failures to his side. *Sorry.* Sorry they weren't better, he seemed to say, mustering up all the gravitas of a military tribunal, seemingly for the audience's benefit.

It is possible that three-plus decades of handing away cash warped Trebek's understanding of money. Sajak, guest-hosting an episode on April Fools' Day 1992, cheerfully called the prior episode's prize of $14,550 "a great day." Trebek himself called a $13,201 payday "modest"; $19,199 became, wistfully, "good enough to remain champion." My hunch is that Trebek seemed willing to settle for his winners making anything above the $20,000-and-change average. More than that and he tended to be reasonably impressed; dip below and he would whip out the knives.

In interviews, Trebek often spoke of his admiration for *Jeopardy!* players' wit, and a viewer might conclude that he presided over the game as an emblem of good sportsmanship: He simply wanted the players to do their very best. But perhaps his determination pointed to something else. A long-simmering contract dispute with Sony? A personal mission to redistribute funds to the world's librarians, art history professors, and ornithologists?

In any case, Trebek would not settle for mediocrity.

Though he might have come to Hollywood seeking show business generally, his pedagogy on *Jeopardy!* wasn't really a part. Fluent in English and French, he also said he could "fool around in" German, Italian, Spanish, and Russian (his father, George, immigrated to Canada from Ukraine). He mentioned his daily crossword habit to me and said, with some satisfaction, that he could get through them all—"even the tough ones on Friday, Saturday."

What about the test for new contestants? I ask. Did he really take it every year?

"I took it for, I don't know, fifteen, twenty years," Trebek says. "I said that when the day came that I failed the test, I would resign as host of the show. Then after that many years I said, 'To hell with it. I've got the job.'"

That doesn't mean, however, that he doesn't consider knowing the answers (and, yes, questions) to be a point of pride. Contestant Ted Berg lost in a 2019 Final Jeopardy! when neither he nor his opponents—Gairen Wallace and then-eighteen-time-champ Jason Zuffranieri, whose reign would finally come to an end in his next game—could come up with the name for the landmark that Mark Twain described "sputtering jets of fire" and "heat from Pele's furnaces."

As the credits rolled, the host—a devoted Twain fan—approached the three contestants, seemingly dismayed that none of them had worked it out. Berg says that he had known it was a Hawaiian volcano, but just couldn't get to Kilauea. "Trebek came over to explain it to us afterward," Berg remembers. "He was telling me, 'Don't you remember seeing those videos of the lava spilling out onto the road?'" For Berg, balm this was not.

As the years passed, Trebek seems to have had the realization that what started as the brisk officiousness of the game-show hosts of yore had started instead to strike audiences as a personality trait. If Trebek had begun his hosting career with the hope of projecting competence, control, and maybe just a *hint* of slick-talking charm, it read to some as the performance of a brusque smart aleck—sometimes fussy or outright mean.

So Trebek set about building it into a character.

In his many cameos on other shows, he mostly played Disappointed Trebek, or Judgmental Trebek, or Insufferable Know-It-All Trebek. He voiced himself on a 1997 episode of *The Simpsons*, sending studio goons—er, "judges"—after poor Marge to extract her negative winnings when a game didn't go her way. More recently, he turned up as an overinvolved guest narrator during a live episode of the sitcom *Hot in Cleveland*, barging in to interrupt two characters struggling to remember the name of the Kathy Bates movie adaptation of a Stephen King novel. "Ooh, sorry, that's wrong," he begins. "The response we wanted was 'What is *Misery?*' Everybody knows that *Fried Green Tomatoes* is from the novel by Fannie Flagg—" He is shooed away at gunpoint. "He is *such* a know-it-all," one of the show's remainders sighs.

He appeared on *The Weird Al Show* in 1997, where he advertised "the Know-it-all Correspondence School." "Would you like to make more money?" he asked. "Impress your friends? Be like me and know everything in the world? Sure you would!"

"He was not afraid to make fun of his persona," Weird Al Yankovic himself remembers. "He totally got the humor and was totally game."

On *Jeopardy!*, watching for cracks in Trebek's steely demeanor became something of a pastime for viewers, something like catching a comedian breaking. During Rogers's 2017 streak, Trebek seemed to make a show of his apparent annoyance. In his first game, the bartender swore repeatedly after missing clues until Trebek finally chided him on air: "You realize, of course, that we will be bleeping two or three of what you've had to say so far this half hour." In response, Rogers chuckled and carried on, defiantly telling Trebek, "That's all right." If they made a good pair, it was by the design of the host, who developed a seasoned sports announcer's sense of when to stay out of the way of the action and let momentum build, and when to jump in and egg his players on.

"I don't mind poking fun at myself," says Trebek—who once, during the finale of the Ultimate Tournament of Champions, opted to cut the tension by emerging onstage (and on camera) without his pants, his dark dress socks pulled up nearly to his knees. "I don't even mind when other people poke fun at me."

What about *Jeopardy!*'s pop-culture and rap clues? I ask. In recent years, the writers seem to have developed a fondness for loosing Trebek on hyper-modern linguistics (a 2017 category—about female monarchs, of course: "Yas, Queen") and especially unusual lyrics—for example, *The Fresh Prince of Bel-Air*'s theme song ("In the theme to this '90s sitcom," said the host before switching to a less-than-fluid staccato, " 'I pulled up to the house about 7 or 8 & I yelled to the cabbie, "Yo, homes, smell ya later!" ' "). Isn't it ever uncomfortable, I wondered, to find himself reading something like, as he did in one episode, "Panda, panda…panda panda panda panda panda"?

"No," Trebek says.

Not at all?

Not at all. For Trebek (and, one supposes, for *Jeopardy!*, or at least for *Jeopardy!*'s social media arm), the strangeness was the goal. The usually studious host made a point of not listening to the songs on clues like these ahead of taping—the better to sound perplexed. "I read the clues in a way that's going to make me look silly and make the audiences laugh.

"I take my job very seriously," he says. "I don't take *myself* too seriously."

In 2010, contestant Sally Ronald used her Q&A segment to tell a story about doing the chicken dance at a minor-league baseball game. Ronald says that Trebek had never heard of the dance—a bobbing, clapping routine meant to evoke the bird, and thus somewhat less dignified than the waltz. "And he responded with a classic Alex 'Oooookay' and moved on to the next contestant," she says.

But then, during a mid-game commercial break, he walked back to Ronald's podium. "So what's this dance again?" he asked.

Ronald explained, and then all of a sudden Trebek was doing it with her, both ducking and flapping their elbows like they didn't have a care in the world.

Like Trebek, Fleming assumed that his own version of *Jeopardy!* would be short-lived. "I thought it might run three months, six months, who knows?" Fleming said. But for both hosts, the show took off. Fleming's version ended when the original host was fifty-one, and he would complain in his later years that the association kept him from getting other gigs. *Jeopardy!* had transformed him: Long after his version had ended and a new host had taken over, he was still expected to have all the answers.

In 1992, when Trebek had already spent the better part of a decade as host, he told a reporter that he was fine staying where he was. "I joke about having them wheel me out in a chair," he said.

Still, he imagined a life post-*Jeopardy!* "But in 20 years I'd like to be living off the fat of the land," he continued, "watching my son as he jumps high and slam dunks or throws the long bomb for Notre Dame."

But twenty years came and went, then most of another decade; his son now runs a restaurant in New York City (and went to Fordham, where he studied philosophy, just like his dad), and he continued to host.

Even bad colds were generally unable to keep Trebek out of the studio. Once, he hosted in the throes of a particular nasty bug. "My voice got so bad that our producer decided it would be a terrible distraction on the air," he remembers, "so I had to go into a sound recording studio and dub myself. Talk about difficult work, trying to synchronize my voice with my lips."

"I don't even do that in real life," he deadpans.

Every few years when his contract came up for renewal, Trebek would make some noise about considering retirement, particularly as he crept into his seventies. If it was a negotiating tactic, it was a good one, as each time, a new contract was his.

So when his diagnosis of pancreatic cancer came in the spring of 2019, it was, among many other things, confusing. Could Trebek actually not intend to spend the rest of this decade, plus the one after that and the one after that, guiding contestants through each day's game? Pancreatic cancer is a monster of a disease, a fact Trebek surely knew from the outset: Fleming himself died of it in 1995, just two weeks after receiving his diagnosis.

Still, Trebek refused to consider a farewell—even as he spoke of going backstage between tapings, doubled over with stomach pain, or as chemotherapy-induced sores in his mouth made enunciating clues suddenly difficult. When his hair began to fall out midway through Season 35's tapings, he challenged viewers to figure out when exactly he started wearing a hairpiece. "Truth told, I have to," he joked of carrying on in a video recorded to announce his illness. "Because under the terms of my contract, I have to host *Jeopardy!* for three more years."

⟵

Every so often—not every day, not every week, but regularly enough—Trebek watched *Jeopardy!* He was droll about it: "I check in from time to time to see if I'm losing it," he tells me, and wastes no time before praising the show's director, who, he insists, makes him look good.

It's got to be a strange thing, Trebek watching *Jeopardy!* after all these years, settling into his living room at 7:00 p.m. just as so many others settle into their own and do the exact same thing. Preparing to shift some past time line— a commanding champion, a close game, a winning streak, a plucky challenger—on into the present. Leaning back into his couch and listening: "*And now, here is the host of* Jeopardy!*, Alex Trebek!*"

In his dressing room, word comes back that the host is needed onstage. I'll watch minutes later as he stands behind his lectern—he, for one, never calls it a podium—at last and rattles off, enunciation perfect, tone warm and inviting and familiar, one right after the other: "*Watch the* Jeopardy! *All-Star Games starting tomorrow.*" "*Watch the* Jeopardy! *All-Star Games starting today.*" "*Which team will take home the $1 million prize?*" "*Hey, it's their last chance to compete for the $1* *million prize.*" The whole room, packed with contestants and crew and onlookers, all but holds its collective breath to keep from interrupting.

Now he stands up from the couch, nods, and darts to the door, grabbing his blazer from a hook on his way out.

CHAPTER FOUR

TIME TO TRAIN

The call arrives from an unknown number with a Los Angeles area code, and somewhere in the pit of your stomach, in a dark, primordial corner of your DNA, you feel the fear before you even feel the joy.

The producer just wants to check a few of your application details, nothing too serious, see if maybe since your audition you've done something silly like get a job with *Wheel of Fortune* or commit a felony. No? Larceny? Nothing? Well then, this is it: There's a spot waiting for you on *Jeopardy!* Dear God, you're going on *Jeopardy!*

"It's such an authority in my household that it was like I was getting a call from the cops," Ted Berg, who played in 2019, remembers of getting the call. "It was like: *Am I being accused of cheating? What have I done?*"

Contestants usually get the call—*The Call!*—inviting them

to a taping somewhere between four and six weeks before their tape day. It could come days after their audition, or it could be many months. *Jeopardy!* says it keeps candidates in the contestant pool for eighteen months after they audition before they need to reapply, but sometimes that window is mysteriously larger: James Holzhauer, for one, got the call twenty-two months after auditioning. But whenever it arrives, it does, and suddenly it's time to train.

"This is the *Moneyball* era of *Jeopardy!*" Ken Jennings told me in the midst of Holzhauer's thirty-two-game winning streak, referring to the 2003 book by Michael Lewis that chronicled attempts by the perennially cash-strapped Oakland Athletics to build a champion by exploiting the inefficiencies of their opponents and of baseball writ large. "People statistically study the game before they go on. They build little simulators or use friends' simulators to get hundreds of hours in the tank, like air force pilots. This did not happen a few years ago when I was on *Jeopardy!* It's a whole new game now for people trying to get on the show, and you see the results of it with somebody like James."

In the weeks before they go on *Jeopardy!*, some players go to extreme lengths to prepare. They rearrange their furniture to resemble a contestant lectern and crank down their thermostats to simulate the studio's chill. They shuffle their sleep and meal schedules to match what they will experience in Los Angeles. They binge episodes and deploy studying tools, some intended for *Jeopardy!* and some not: digital flash card programs like Anki and Quizlet, the trivia website Sporcle, buzzer simulators and apps that pull from the reservoir of past clues at the J! Archive. They pore over books and articles written by past *Jeopardy!* champs and seek them out on Reddit and the *Jeopardy!* message board JBoard. They wear uncomfortable shoes; they stand on boxes; they fly in out-of-state friends for mock games; they toss and turn.

Take it from the contestants of Season 36. Berg blew off work to make opera flash cards. Miriam Manber, an attorney, dedicated herself to mastering game theory. Traci Mack enlisted her husband, a Google engineer, to build a realistic buzzer apparatus, LED lights and all; he played host while night after night, she played full games of *Jeopardy!* as an algorithm he designed measured her reaction time. Kris Sunderic slowly weaned himself off coffee so that the cup he planned to have in the green room would have maximum effect.

"I donated $20 to Wikipedia for the first time today," Aravind Byju told me weeks before he taped, "after an ad popped up: 'We see you've been using Wikipedia a lot lately…'"

Lynn Yu didn't wait for the call to start her preparations: Within days of her audition in August 2019, she launched what she called "Road to *Jeopardy!*: A 365-Day Regimen for the Idiot Maniac," an exhaustive plan for mental and physical preparation that she detailed in weekly installments online. Some were obvious enough—score her practice games and seek out unfamiliar movies and music that might fall under *Jeopardy!*'s domain—while others seemed more in keeping with something decidedly more athletic than a quiz show: She cut alcohol, started drinking a Tom Brady–inspired smoothie each morning, and began training for a 15k. "I'm treating *Jeopardy!* like it's a sport," she said. "Like it's something I need to physically train for."

"It's become the focus of everything I do," Hemant Mehta said as his taping neared. "I don't care about the money. I know this is so reality-TV-cliché, but I want the title. For *Jeopardy!*, if I win with $1, that would be a dream come true."

Not all *Jeopardy!* contestants immerse themselves in preparation in the weeks before they go on the show. After all, they nabbed one of those elusive four hundred spots in a given season with whatever was already in their brain.

But many do. Here, we'll dig into two of the fundamental areas of preparation: the buzzer and subject matter.

THE BUZZER

The way the buzzer works on *Jeopardy!* today is seemingly designed to confound anxious bookworms.

The 1960s and 1970s iteration of *Jeopardy!* was a more chaotic experience than the show we know today. Contestants were allowed to ring in as early as they liked, even if the host hadn't finished reading the clue, leading to frequent confusion over who had control of the board. Worse, it ruined the experience of playing along from home. How were you supposed to prove your *Jeopardy!* mettle if those nerds in the studio were *ding*-ing in before you could even finish reading?

So by the second year of the Alex Trebek–helmed revival, *Jeopardy!* changed the rule, introducing the system that still exists today.

Now, after each clue is selected, the host reads its entire text aloud. The moment the last word is finished, a dedicated *Jeopardy!* staffer sitting at the judges' table just offstage— Michael Harris, who also serves as one of the show's senior researchers—manually activates a switch that illuminates blue lights alongside the outer edges of the *Jeopardy!* board. The moment the "enable light" switches on, the three onstage contestants are permitted to ring in, but if they press their buzzers even a fraction of a beat too early, they will be locked out of the system for one-quarter of a second, which is generally enough time for an opponent to swoop in instead. It's a mechanism that's hidden from viewers—you can't see the blue lights in the telecast. (Harris isn't the only one who wears multiple hats on the *Jeopardy!* set. Even co–head writer Michele Loud has another duty, serving as the backup scorekeeper while games tape and tallying the scores in real time with paper and pencil.)

The rule change was a significant one: Suddenly, buzzer speed—or more specifically buzzer precision—was a significant element of the game. Compare it, for example, to quiz bowl, long a feeder of *Jeopardy!* contestants. Like *Jeopardy!*, quiz bowl prides itself on its demanding material; unlike *Jeopardy!*, it is aggressively spectator-unfriendly.

Quiz bowl does allow for early ringing in, à la early *Jeopardy!* Much of the competition, in fact, turns on just how early you can interrupt the moderator: Responses can be worth more if players buzz in and answer correctly before a certain point in the question. In many cases, the moderator awards a team points and then moves on without so much as bothering to finish reading the question.

But for *Jeopardy!*, the strategy shift was worth the entertainment gains. "Some *Jeopardy!* fans argue that this change altered a basic tenet of the strategy," Trebek wrote of the rule change in *The Jeopardy! Book*, six years after his version debuted, "but one has to realize that we are producing a television show, not simply an in-studio quiz for contestants. It is vital that the home viewer participates in the program, or there is no program."

The result? On *Jeopardy!*, the buzzer is king.

Jennings puts it this way: "Almost all of the contestants know almost all of the answers almost all of the time," he says. Which is to say that more often than not, all three players know a given clue's answer, and all three are attempting to ring in—meaning buzzer timing is hugely important.

"If you put random people up there on *Jeopardy!*, the most important thing would be who knows the answers," says Jennings. "But with players that good, buzzer timing really becomes what tends to separate the winner from the nonwinners."

Jennings should know: His original stint on *Jeopardy!*— that seventy-four-game winning spree—was such a display of technical dominance that midway through his run, the show's powers that be changed the practice itinerary for new players to make things easier on those attempting to unseat a champion. (The show claims it was an unrelated change—but, well...)

New players have always begun their tape days with a practice round while the contestant coordinators gently course-correct those they notice are ringing in too early or too late, or holding the buzzer in a position likely to get them in trouble. (Maggie Speak long advised against what she called the "Statue of Liberty pose," which she suggested might get tiring over the course of a half-hour episode.) But unlike during the first part of Jennings's run, this practice round now also includes the actual in-game buzzer operator—Harris—at the enable-light switchboard instead of a rehearsal stand-in, giving challengers a crucial chance to familiarize themselves with his light-up tempo.

Jennings isn't the only dominant champion to experience a change in buzzer procedures midway through a winning streak. In 2021, Matt Amodio returned to the *Jeopardy!* set following the show's annual summer hiatus to defend his then-18-game streak—and discovered that new contestants now begin their mornings with two practice sessions instead of the previous season's one. As in Jennings's case, *Jeopardy!* says that the change was unrelated to Amodio or any other contestant—and indeed, both players kept winning with the new policies. *Jeopardy!*, for its part, maintains that the new procedure offers the same amount of practice as the old policy. But the shift caught the champ by surprise all the same.

"They didn't say anything about it," Amodio says. "When we got there for the new season we were doing a rehearsal and then they said, 'OK, now we'll do our second rehearsal.' And I'm like, 'Uhh…'"

"In general, I think that opponents should have as much buzzer practice as possible until I win, and then they should have no buzzer practice," Amodio jokes.

The *Jeopardy!* buzzer is a decidedly weird piece of machinery, both wider in circumference and heavier than you'd think it would be. Many aspiring players fashion their own versions to practice ringing in with at home: Jennings used one of his son's toys, while others use ballpoint pens—with many opting for the red-topped, blue-gripped version given out by the contestant crew at auditions. Holzhauer made his own, wrapping a thick layer of masking tape around a mechanical pencil.

"I would save several episodes to watch back-to-back on my

DVR," Holzhauer says, "and when I had an hour free from work and parenting, I'd put on dress shoes to simulate standing that way during the tape day," clicking his pencil-buzzer as needed.

Those who do master the buzzer sometimes struggle to explain how they've done it. Michael McKean, for example, wonders if an old thumb injury helped his buzzer abilities during his *Celebrity Jeopardy!* outings. As an acting student in college, he was required to take a rotation on the stage crew; while building a set, he passed his right hand too close to the end of a table saw. "The crew chief showed up at the hospital with the end of my thumb wrapped in a hankey," he says, "but it was too small to reassemble."

The result: McKean has what he calls his "funky thumb," which is notably wider than the one on his left hand. He also tends to double-tap the buzzer when he rings in. "I don't know why I do that," he says—but in any case, he has won every *Celebrity Jeopardy!* game he's been a part of, as well as a celebrity episode of *Rock & Roll Jeopardy!*

Different schools of thought have emerged on how best to deal with buzzer timing. Some players, like Jennings, go mostly by sound: If you get the host's rhythm in your head, you can get a pretty good sense of when enable-light operator Harris—who's doing precisely the same thing in that moment—is going to hit the switch. This strategy has some drawbacks, such as during the show's frequent use of alternative readers of clues, be they Clue Crew members or celebrities promoting a themed category. Says 2009 Tournament of Champions winner Dan Pawson, "The worst is when it's an audio clue and Alex isn't talking. We're all waiting for the lights like animals."

For long-returning champions who cut their teeth with Trebek, an additional element of uncertainty loomed about the future: When, someday, the show had a different host, would their hard-won timing mastery be sent back to square one?

Other players—including Holzhauer—have been drawn more to the science than the art of buzzing in, leaning on the same sort of analytics-based approach that dictated his Daily Double hunting. For these players, there is a sacred text: *Secrets of the Buzzer,* by Fritz Holznagel.

Holznagel first competed on *Jeopardy!* in 1994. At the time, he didn't worry much about the buzzer and won four games, a stint that led to invitations to three subsequent *Jeopardy!* tournaments, most recently the 2014 Battle of the Decades. "When I got invited back for the Battle of the Decades, I was fifty-two years old," Holznagel says. "I knew that I was not really in the loop on pop culture, and just generally, there's no way you're going to be smarter than these other contestants. It occurred to me that if I was going to have any hope of doing well in this tournament, I would have to find some other edge."

That edge he went about sharpening? Buzzer reaction time. *Jeopardy!*, he says, is a unique beast in the trivia world. "If you're playing a College Bowl or quiz bowl or that kind of thing, people can ring in anytime," he says. "But *Jeopardy!* is really unusual and different and it has this one twist, which is it's basically a reaction-time test tacked onto a trivia contest." He wondered: Could he hack it?

With the help of some friends, he created a wired buzzer that timed his buzzing speed, and over the course of some twenty-seven thousand tests, he managed to lower his reaction time from 228 milliseconds to as low as 126 milliseconds.

Holznagel's trials led him to a series of general guidelines for buzzer mastery: Use the thumb of your dominant hand, keep your arms in front of you, hold still, and—if you can—chug some coffee in the backstage green room. Oh: And keep your eyes locked on the about-to-be-illuminated enable light.

JAMES HOLZHAUER, BUZZER WUNDERKIND

"He had a lot of questions about the subtlety of the buzzer right away," Maggie Speak told me.

Before her Season 36 retirement, Speak led the hour-long group orientation for new players each tape day, including the first one that featured James Holzhauer. "Before he ever hit the stage, it was: 'Well, what if I do this?' He had a lot of very specific questions about the timing of the buzzer.

"And clearly my answers must have helped him," she added, laughing. Indeed: Over the course of his winning streak, he rang in first an astonishing 57.81 percent of the time, according to analysis by *The Jeopardy! Fan*—a hair behind the mark of Ken Jennings, widely considered perhaps the most prodigious buzzer in the game's history, who managed 59.31 percent through the same point in his own streak.

Principally, Holzhauer wanted to know about the quarter-second lockout penalty players face if they ring in too early. If he rang in early multiple times, would the quarter seconds stack on top of each other? Could he find himself locked out for half a second, three-quarters of a second—egads, even a full second, by which point both his opponents would surely have had their own chance to ring in? (No, the penalties do not stack. Some successful *Jeopardy!* alumni, like Jerome Vered, recommend going so far as to practice ringing in at intervals of a quarter second: That way, if you get locked out, you'll have learned to buzz in at the precise moment that your buzzer is re-enabled. Speak discourages this, saying that it's more likely to confuse stressed-out contestants—but it's certainly worked for Vered, who's racked up $499,102 across four stints on the show.)

The aptly named Buzzy Cohen—a three-time contestant and winner of the 2017 Tournament of Champions—was in the *Jeopardy!* studio audience during one of Holzhauer's first games and saw his buzzer mastery up close. "It was kind of like there was no one else up there," Cohen says.

"It's like when a great hockey player is playing, or a great basketball player," he continues. "There aren't defenders. There's nothing between them and the goal or them and the hoop—that's what it feels like at times. You know there are people standing there, but they just kind of move through them."

Holzhauer had had some practice. He had

previously competed at Trivia Nationals, Cohen says, "and he has won the 5x5 competition there, which is a very similar game to *Jeopardy!*, but instead of three contestants, it's five contestants. So you can imagine having to buzz in faster than twice as many competitors."

Holzhauer's reliance on Fritz Holznagel's wisdom—and specifically Holznagel's advice to time a buzz to the illumination of the blue enable light around the board, *not* the sound of Alex Trebek's voice reading the clue—sets him apart from other *Jeopardy!* champions, the vast majority of whom insist that buzzing by sound is the only way to win. Noting that contestant coordinators recommended the lights approach when he first played, 1996 Tournament of Champions winner Michael Dupée vehemently disagreed in his book, *How to Get on Jeopardy! and Win!* "If you do that you will not win," he wrote. "I have never heard of a Tournament of Champions competitor who relied on those lights (and I have talked to twenty of them)."

More than a few *Jeopardy!* champs have voiced to me that they don't think Holzhauer *really* waits for the lights—the sort of nerdy conspiracy theory that could perhaps only arise around a show like *Jeopardy!*

At any rate, Holzhauer didn't just compete in the 2019 Tournament of Champions—he won. Months later, however, he fell to Jennings in the Greatest of All Time tournament, perhaps a vindication for the buzz-by-sound school (though he did, along with Jennings, succeed in boxing out Brad Rutter, also a buzz-by-sound-er and in previous tournaments usually the fastest buzz in the West, but who this time was able to ring in first just 17.11 percent of the time, according to *The Jeopardy! Fan*). Was this a verdict on the superiority of the sound strategy, or is Jennings just that good on the buzzer? And if the lights strategy is actually holding Holzhauer back, is it possible that if he returns to play again in the future, he could switch to playing by sound and become even faster?

Holzhauer admits that he tried out voice timing as he prepared for GOAT. "But I wasn't noticing any tangible improvement," he says. By the time the tournament began, he says he "started to play by feel": "Batting practice is no substitute for facing actual hundred-mile-per-hour fastballs, and in-game adjustments during my first few games were very helpful."

His loss had not made him rethink his reliance on the lights. "I got in first my share of the time against the two greatest buzzer-wielders of all time," Holzhauer says. "If anything, that reinforces the efficacy of my approach."

Buzzing in isn't the most important thing on *Jeopardy!*, of course. Holzhauer could have been the first to buzz in on every clue and make Daily Double wagers just as calculated as he did, but if he didn't know the answers, that would have gotten him nowhere.

Still: "If you're not in control of the board, if you're not calling the clues, you don't get to make those big bets on the Daily Double," says Cohen. "So in order to make sure you're in control you need to be answering questions correctly, and the best way to do that is by buzzing in first.

"And knowing stuff," he adds.

At Trivia Nationals, Holznagel has become something of a celebrity. In 2019, he went so far as to host what he called a "buzzinar": part breakdown of *Secrets of the Buzzer*, part Q&A, and part real-time buzzer trial.

Before Holzhauer's winning streak, Holznagel's book had been something less than a bestseller. "I published it in 2015 and kind of forgot about it," he says. "I put it on Amazon and it sold seventy or eighty copies over the next few years."

But then *Jeopardy!* James happened—Holznagel calls him "the big dog"—and went around telling journalists that Holznagel's book had helped him win. Suddenly everyone wanted to know the *Secrets of the Buzzer*—so much so that Holznagel put out a second edition with a brand-new foreword by the big dog himself.

At the buzzinar, Holznagel enlists a guinea pig—a *Jeopardy!* and buzzer novice named Carlo—to try a few rounds of ringing in on his homemade buzzer system. Carlo's speed is so-so: about 313 milliseconds. Holznagel hands him an enormous cup of lukewarm coffee—the better for chugging, though it does not look, based on Carlo's facial expressions, particularly appetizing—and tells him to drink. Consuming caffeine, says Holznagel, is one of the very best things a contestant can do to speed up their buzzer timing. In his book, he credits it with shaving five one-thousandths of a second off his reaction time, a razor-thin margin as dazzling here as it might be at an Olympic trial.

"Any particular blend, like Sumatran, or ...?" someone asks.

A semicircle of *Jeopardy!* hopefuls surrounds Holznagel and Carlo, and they want specifics. What about freeze-dried coffee? Iced? Does tea work? Holznagel fields the questions as best he can—caffeine, any caffeine, should do the trick, though espresso is actually less effective, and tea *should* work, though he can't say for sure—as people across the room furiously take notes. "Can you do crack?" another person asks, and laughs break out; "There actually is a section on amphetamines," Holznagel replies, sheepishly. (He does not recommend them.)

Holznagel lists attributes that he claims, with the hearty asterisk that he does not have a medical background, slow reaction time down. Most of these, alas, cannot be helped: being under twenty, over fifty, drunk, an introvert, or right-handed. Female, too, makes the list, and Holznagel is apologetic as he says so: The studies he's gleaned all this from aren't his, they're old and not *Jeopardy!*-specific, and things are slowly getting better—he does not say how—but, well, he can only share what he has read. "You said the buzzer is our friend," one woman calls out, sounding betrayed. "The buzzer is *sexist*."

No less than Maggie Speak sat in on the buzzinar, seemingly bemused by the militancy of her future contestants. "I think people are afraid of the buzzer," she says. "It's a common thing we hear: *This is not working.* They psych themselves out."

Toward the end, Holznagel's guinea pig reapproaches the buzzer. This time, giant cup drained, he was down to 197 milliseconds—a spectacular reduction that impresses even Holznagel. The room launches into a round of applause.

Somewhere in between the pro-lights, anti-sound camp and the pro-sound, anti-lights camp lies a third school on buzzer timing that advises a bit of both. Says Jennifer Quail, who won eight games in 2020, and was runner-up in the following year's Tournament of Champions, of her technique: It was a "semi-Zen state of listening for the last word in the clue while keeping soft eyes on the lights."

After I joke that that doesn't sound difficult at all, she adds, "It's hard to describe, but that's as close as I can come to the feeling of thinking about what I was doing while not thinking too much about it."

Ben Ingram, another eight-time champ as well as the winner of the 2014 Tournament of Champions, did something unusual while he was playing: He changed his strategy midway through a game. He says that he was "voice all the way" through his initial run and well into the Tournament of Champions. But when he reached the All-Star Games in 2019, he found he could no longer get through—so he switched to waiting for the lights, and says he suddenly found that he was winning buzzer battles 40 percent of the time, an extremely high mark on *Jeopardy!* when facing seasoned opponents.

Ingram suspects that it might have had something to do with who he was playing: "Couldn't beat them at their game so [had to] try something else," he says.

Still other contestants insist that the pursuit of buzzer perfection is a lost cause. "It's a person," Amodio says of the in-game buzzer operator, "and that means that the buzzer timing that you have to match is not exactly the same every time. So even if you were somehow a perfectly tuned musician who's on rhythm every single time, your target is moving so you're not going to be perfect in terms of matching it every time. There's a lot of variability to that that's beyond your control."

As buzzer strategy has gone mainstream, so too has trying to find an edge over opponents, particularly in reunion tournaments among players who've made repeated appearances on the *Jeopardy!* stage. The 2017 Houston Astros this is not, but with hundreds of thousands of dollars on the line in major tournaments, champs might take a look at the tape— that is, their opponents' previous *Jeopardy!* outings—to try to piece together what the competition might have up their sleeves.

Adds Ingram, maybe in jest or maybe not: "If someone asks what you do, lie."

SUBJECT MATTER

A curiously pervasive misconception about *Jeopardy!* is that players are given a study guide before they play, something that lays out the categories they're about to face. The reality is that no such thing occurs—and that this would in fact be a federal crime, thanks to our old pal Charles Van Doren. Instead, players have as much of an idea of what they'll be seeing as you do when you switch the evening's episode on.

So, for the player looking to study ahead of time, that simply leaves the entirety of the Western canon, plus the occasional step beyond it. What trouble could that pose?

A pair of excellent guides to *Jeopardy!* material were written in the 1990s by former champions—*Secrets of the Jeopardy! Champions* by Chuck Forrest and Mark Lowenthal, and *How to Get on Jeopardy! and Win!* by Michael Dupée—and together they provide a solid primer on the *Jeopardy!* classics that still pop up regularly: presidential history, geography, Canada (no, really).

More important, perhaps, is what they tell us about *Jeopardy!* material as a whole. A central thesis of both might be this: While *Jeopardy!* expects its contestants to know about a great many things, the show only really asks a handful of relatively superficial things about each. You might, for example, be expected to know the names of Franklin D. Roosevelt's beloved Scottish Terrier, notable cousin, last vice president, or the international park where he spent his summers, but you're probably *not* going to be asked for his dog's original name. The goal is to build a surface-level amount of knowledge about a wide array of subjects.

(Your FDR answers: Fala; Theodore *or* Eleanor—ahem; Harry Truman; Campobello; Big Boy. Roosevelt renamed him "Murray the Outlaw of Falahill" after a Scottish ancestor memorialized in a ballad for thumbing his nose at King James IV—Fala for short.)

Holzhauer prepared for his appearance on the show by using a tried-and-true technique: studying children's books, which tend to condense complicated topics down to their most vital and interesting facts. (He favored Zachary Hamby's books on mythology and *Classics Illustrated*, a long-running series that transformed literary classics into digestible comics. Jane Eyre, for example, pulls no punches: "I married him," she says plainly of her beloved Mr. Rochester.)

This strategy was actually pioneered by the show's writers. In *Jeopardy!*'s earliest years, the writers overcame the shortfalls of their then-limited physical library at the studio by assigning each writer and researcher a weekly "library day" to go visit the real thing. Kids' books became a favorite way to parse far-flung subjects and track down the sort of obscure-but-interesting factoids that are *Jeopardy!*'s bread and butter.

Many champions recommend memorizing lists of frequently recurring categories—things like world capitals, cocktails (that is, potent potables), First Ladies, vice presidents, Shakespearean characters, college towns and mascots, state nicknames, and Academy Award winners. Then there are what the trivia community calls Pavlovs: descriptors that almost always pair with a specific answer, providing a shortcut to those who memorize them. If, for example, an art clue mentions soup cans, you can bet that it's looking for Andy Warhol, and anytime a Finnish composer comes up, it's exceedingly likely to be Jean Sibelius. Memorize the keywords—Hungarian divorcée equals Zsa Zsa Gabor, Menlo Park equals Thomas Edison—and you can get a jump on your opponents.

A BRIEF HISTORY OF *JEOPARDY!* CONTESTANTS KNOWING NOTHING ABOUT SPORTS

Let the record show that nerds can be jocks, and that jocks can be nerds. A mathlete can be a quarterback; a point guard, a Model UN delegate. But every so often, the very smart people who turn up on *Jeopardy!* also happen to be the sort of people who refer to baseball, basketball, and the like as "sportsball."

I can say nothing as to their collective memories of PE, though I can say that I once heard a well-respected and multiple-event-winning player at Trivia Nationals hiss under his breath that he could not and would not bring himself to study, much less *watch*, sporting events, despite having identified sports as the single biggest hole in his trivia knowledge base. "It's like watching paint dry," he sighed.

On *Jeopardy!*, contestants have named Texas A&M Heisman winner Johnny Manziel an Alabama star and Babe Ruth as the player who broke Major League Baseball's color barrier. They have posited 191 as a feasible number of home runs hit in a single season, stared stonily at a demonstration of a changeup, and identified both Wrigley Field and Comiskey Park as the home of the Red Sox. In 2017, three contestants staggered their way through an "NFL Teams by Hall of Famer" category, which saw one player buzz in to guess the Colorado Rockies. ("No, sorry," Trebek said, patiently.)

In 2014, one contestant credited Magic Johnson with having eleven 100-plus-assist seasons in the NHL. "Oh no," said Trebek, his Canadian veneer cracking ever so slightly; the *Washington Post* wrote it up as "Magic Johnson. What Is Worst *Jeopardy!* Answer Ever?" (A second contestant supplied the right answer: Wayne Gretzky. "We're talking about *hockey*, not the NBA," said Trebek.)

Jeopardy! contestants don't always fail at sports clues. In 2015, players whizzed through the categories "Sports Lingo" and "Baseball Stadiums"; in 2018, a trio made quick work of "NHL Logos."

But then you have cases like the one in 2010, when Meg Miller, who entered Final Jeopardy! in the lead, named the "Jacksonville Panthers" as the only NFC team to have never made it to the Super Bowl. "I don't actually care," she said, shrugging as Trebek offered, politely, "It's the Jacksonville *Jaguars*, I believe." (Correct answer: the Detroit Lions.) But she'd seen the category—"Super Bowl"—and bet accordingly: She lost just $1,000, and won the game.

And then there was the Great Football Talkin'. In the Jeopardy! round—the, *ahem*, intentionally easier half—of a 2018 game, players Ryan Fenster, Justin Earnshaw, and Sara Helmers worked their way across the board. They cleared one category, and then another, and then a third, fourth, and fifth, until all that remained were the five clues in the round's last remaining column: "Talkin' Football."

With palpable reluctance, they began.

The contestants didn't know what an option play was. ("Your choice: Do or don't name this play in which the QB runs the ball & can choose to pitch it to another back.") They didn't know what offsetting penalties were. ("These 'penalties' are simultaneous violations by the offense & defense that cancel each other out.") They didn't know which team Tom Landry coached, or what a fair catch was (Trebek attempted to mime one for them afterward, in the apparent hope of belated enrichment). And they definitely didn't know who the Purple People Eaters were.

"I can tell you guys are big football fans," Trebek said the first time his contestants blanked. He had no idea. By the time they reached the category's last clue, the host had a threat: "If you guys ring in and get this one," he told them, "*I will die.*"

In the end, Fenster, Earnshaw, and Helmers completed one of *Jeopardy!*'s rarest and most ignominious feats: a so-called triple stumper— clues for which none of the three contestants offers a correct answer—through the entirety of a category.

Indeed, they went even further: They did not

so much as ring in for a single clue. They did not even do that thing that players sometimes do, scrunching up their faces like the answer is just on the tip of their tongue. They didn't wave their fists when the right answer was revealed to indicate that they should've known. No: The three contestants listened to each clue and then stood in silence, fidgeting and looking bashful until the *boop-boop-boop* timer rang. They did this five times. It was, in a word, spectacular.

Fenster, who ultimately won the game, didn't seem too torn up about it. When he returned to the stage for the 2019 Tournament of Champions, he recorded a promo: "I'm Ryan Fenster, and I'm ready for any category," he said, "as long as it's not 'Talkin' Football.'"

Trebek, too, seemed to get a kick out of the category. For a game in early 2020, he personally wrote a sequel category. "Now, last year, we had some difficulty with the football category, so we thought we would try it again," the host explained. "But in this category, it deals entirely with referees' signals, and I'm going to be giving you three players the signal."

So he did, thoughtfully demonstrating holding fouls and touchdowns. This time, the players rang in for each clue, though they weren't always right. "All right, we got about half of them there," said Trebek. "Let's go somewhere else."

By the time Roger Craig—no relation to the running back—got the call in 2010, one month after his third audition, he was certain of one thing: The best source of reference material is the show itself. *Jeopardy!* is now more than eight thousand episodes into its current edition, and while the writers aim to build gaps between repeating information, some recirculation, both of facts (clues) and of subjects (categories), is inevitable. *Jeopardy!* asked about the state where Abraham Lincoln was born in a 1987 game, for example—and then again in 1994, 2002, and 2017. (That'd be Kentucky.) While brand-new topics surface regularly, particularly on the pop-culture front, the *Jeopardy!* canon is a mostly static thing. As Carlo Panno, who met his wife while competing on the Art Fleming edition of the show and who was a researcher in the early years of the Trebek revival, once put it: "They say there are only nine different plots, and I believe there are only about 10,000 *Jeopardy!* clues." Studying old games, therefore, is the single best way to figure out what *Jeopardy!* writers think a player should know.

But the problem for Craig was that there was just too much of it to work with—no one could master *all* of it. Not that that's stopped players from trying: Matt Jackson, who won thirteen games in his original stint on the show, made 364,878 flash cards to prepare for his run in the All-Star Games. (His team, helmed by Jennings and filled out by 2012 College Championship winner Monica Thieu, came in second.)

No such thing would be possible for Craig, however. He'd helped friends prepare for their own *Jeopardy!* tapings, which had led him to become acutely aware of the limits of cramming. "One of the pieces of feedback that I got was that if you wait until you get the call, well, then you only have four or five weeks and you can't learn so much in four or five weeks," Craig says. "If you want to be more prepared, you have to do it over a longer period of time."

So Craig, who was in the midst of a doctorate in computer science when he was tapped to play, did something unusual: He downloaded the entirety of *Jeopardy!*

Okay, not exactly—but pretty close. He turned to the J! Archive.

Craig was after specifics. "Everybody has an idea about what's on the show, but I wanted to try to make it as quantitative as possible," he says. "We all know presidents and Shakespeare come up, but what is the actual percentage of questions about Shakespeare or presidents or world capitals?"

He gathered all the clues then in the J! Archive—about 250,000, he estimates. (These days, the database holds closer to four hundred thousand.) By grouping them together, he was able to build what he calls "a map of the territory of the game"—a method known as knowledge tracking. He likens the result to something like the SAT, where you might be informed ahead of time of the test's breakdown: 10 percent trigonometry, 10 percent algebra. With real *Jeopardy!* clue distribution data in hand, you could pinpoint specific areas to study and identify those most (and least) likely to get you in trouble.

But more important, you could see, by looking at where different subjects tended to appear in games, which weak areas actually matter and decide what to study accordingly. Opera, for example—a bête noire for so many contestants that *Jeopardy!* has named categories "Uh-Oh, Opera" and "The Dreaded Opera Category"—is worthwhile, according to

Craig: While it doesn't come up that often, when it does, it's disproportionately located in high-value positions.

Compare that with nursery rhymes, another recurring *Jeopardy!* topic. "They're never really the Final Jeopardy!s or the tough Daily Double, high-dollar-amount questions, because"—Craig supposes of the writers—"they think those things should be reserved for more esoteric matters."

Craig compares it to football. The little things do matter, he says: "You should be really good at converting fourth downs or getting a first down." But other things are still more important. "These goal-line plays—scoring a touchdown or preventing a touchdown—can swing the game much more than if you've moved the ball three yards down the field."

In the end, Craig won six games as well as the 2011 Tournament of Champions; in his second game, he hit a personal high of $77,000—then the highest one-day total in *Jeopardy!* history.

And indeed, Craig's run, with its strategy driven by the ruthless pursuit of numerical truth, was widely compared to *Moneyball*.

Craig accepts that it's a reasonable comparison. But unlike in baseball, you won't be privy to the weaknesses and inefficiencies of your fellow players in normal *Jeopardy!* gameplay. You can, however, identify your own and do your best to overcome them before you head to the studio, Craig argues. "If you really don't know subject X, you don't have to go become an expert on it," he says. "You just have to fill it in enough that it's not a totally crippling weakness for you, because then your opponents could exploit that."

So confident was Craig in the numbers that he has repeatedly stepped into the land of *Jeopardy!* heresy, endangering leads—sometimes substantial ones—to go all in on a subject that his studying told him he would get right. It happened in his very first game, when he found the first Daily Double of Double Jeopardy! in the $2,000 clue of a category devoted to the periodic table. Craig had done his undergraduate degree in biochemistry, and he'd gone so far as to tell friends beforehand that if he somehow found himself in this position with a chemistry category, he would wager everything. "I don't know it perfectly," he says of the periodic table, "but for *Jeopardy!* purposes, I think I know it very, very well."

And so, despite having just a narrow lead at the time, he went for a true Daily Double, gambling his entire $12,400 and flummoxing Trebek. (The exchange, as recorded in the J! Archive: "Roger: *I'll bet it all. Bet it all.* Alex: [Looking surprised] *Okay, you caught me by surprise.* Roger: *Yeah.* Alex: *Possible big payday for you if you are right on this clue.*") Craig got it, just as he thought he would: Pd, he knew, is the symbol for palladium.

"Roger bets *crazy*," fellow champion Jerome Vered will tell me later, with what sounds like a mix of admiration and horror. Craig's bets are certainly riskier than the average *Jeopardy!* contestant's—in the finals of the Tournament of Champions, he found back-to-back Daily Doubles and went all in both times, sealing his victory and sending a nation of nerds into conniptions. But as Craig would contend, those bets weren't crazy at all. They were just what the numbers said to do.

WHAT WAS THE BEST GAME
OF *JEOPARDY!* EVER?

Among the sort of *Jeopardy!* fans who know that advanced *Jeopardy!* statistics exist, one number is supreme: the Coryat score. Named for Karl Coryat, the 1996 two-time champion who first devised it, it's as close as *Jeopardy!* has to baseball's Weighted Runs Created metric—a pure analysis of offensive contributions.

The score is derived by adding up the value of all the clues that a player answered, right (positive) and wrong (negative), while ignoring any wagering bonuses added (or subtracted, if answered incorrectly) beyond the actual clue value on Daily Doubles. Final Jeopardy!, where the clue's worth is inherently variable, is ignored, as are incorrect Daily Doubles, since the player who picks that clue is forced to answer whether they would normally have rung in or not. If, for example, the only clues I buzzed in on during my game were the six $200 clues in the Jeopardy! round and I was right every time, my Coryat score would be $1,200. If an opponent beat me to one and got it instead, it would be $1,000; if I buzzed in on all six but missed one, it would be $800.

By lopping off the betting component of the game, you can get a sense of how much of the board material a player knew, and a better idea of how well an individual player performed than by simply looking at their dollar total. (This in turn has made the Coryat score a favorite tool for players-to-be hoping to analyze their own at-home, pen-clicking performances.)

You might not be surprised to learn that the ten highest Coryat scores in *Jeopardy!* history are split among Matt Amodio, James Holzhauer, Ken Jennings, and Amy Schneider—the owners of the show's four longest winning streaks. Jennings holds the top spot with $39,200, a mark reached during the seventh game of his 2004 winning streak. His actual cash winnings that day: $50,000.

The Coryat score also helps us answer our question: What was the best—or at least best-played—game of *Jeopardy!* ever?

"If life ever had a way of telling you this was not meant to be—you're going up against the most dominant champion of all time and someone who wrote her master's thesis on *Jeopardy!* questions?" Jay Sexton says. "You just throw up your hands and clap: Whatcha gonna do?"

You might not know Sexton's name, but you likely know who he is. On March 12, 2019, he walked into the Sony studio intent on checking off a lifelong goal of appearing on *Jeopardy!* Sexton, a senior research engineer at Georgia Tech, had spent two decades trying to get there, first trying out in college and then getting into the habit of taking the online contestant test almost every year. He even watched as his sister Susan got her own chance to play in 2016. (She came in third.)

But now that he was finally in the *Jeopardy!* green room, he ran into a problem. Sexton and the other new contestants were introduced to a polite thirty-four-year-old from Las Vegas named James, who sheepishly informed his challengers that he'd racked up thirty-two wins and $2.4 million so far.

Holzhauer's episodes wouldn't start airing for another couple of weeks, so no one outside the studio had yet seen the player who'd been averaging almost $80,000 a game—a smidge below what had previously been Roger Craig's one-day record. "We thought they were pulling our legs," Sexton says. "Like they'd gotten together with the champion and said, 'Hey, let's freak the newbies out a little bit.'"

For Sexton, things only got worse. When names were selected to determine who would play that day's first game, Sexton heard his own alongside Emma Boettcher's. Boettcher, a librarian at the University of Chicago, had indeed written her thesis on *Jeopardy!* questions, and Sexton had noted her in the morning practice session as a particularly dangerous player. "You're eyeing everybody, you're sizing 'em up," Sexton says. "After watching her practice I was thinking, *Wow, that Emma—I'd hate to go up against her, too.*"

If he was going to have any chance at all, he told himself as he walked onto the stage, he would have to do a few not-so-easy things: "I'm going to have to be smart, I'm going to have to be good on the buzzer, and then when I get a Daily Double, I'm going to have to bet possibly uncomfortably large numbers to keep up."

You perhaps know what happened next. Boettcher dominated the game, putting Holzhauer on the back foot and then sending the owner of *Jeopardy!*'s second-longest winning streak home at last. Sexton came in third; all three Daily Doubles were ultimately claimed by his opponents and he confesses he had trouble mastering the buzzer.

But while Boettcher's conquest made headlines, the trio's game is likely to endure in the *Jeopardy!* pantheon for another reason: It was a single answer shy of perfection, making it the best-played *Jeopardy!* game ever.

A personal Coryat score is an imperfect measure of *Jeopardy!* skill, since a player's ability to out-buzz their opponents determines whether they get the chance to offer an answer at all. To get around that, you can use what's called the combined Coryat— all three players' Coryat scores added together—to get an aggregate sense of how well a given game was played.

The highest possible combined Coryat score is $54,000, which would require the three players to answer every single clue correctly: No wrong answers by anyone (which would mean a value subtracted from a player's personal Coryat, and thus also from the total), and no clues left unanswered. It has never happened before—*Jeopardy!* is hard by design.

But by the time Sexton, Boettcher, and Holzhauer hit the first commercial break, they knew they had something special going. "We got to the end of the first round," Sexton says, "and James turned to us and said, 'Wow, y'all, we aced that round.'"

Sexton was responsible for the lone whiff, deciding to guess on a $400 clue in Double Jeopardy! when he realized neither Boettcher nor Holzhauer was going to ring in on it (a triple stumper would also have cost them the perfect bid): "Paternalism is restricting freedom in our (supposed) best interests, like state taxes on these, which began in Iowa in 1921." "I was like, 'Are we really going to lose our perfect game on a top-line clue?'" He now refers to the clue in question as "the stupid, infamous cigarettes question." (He guessed sales tax.)

In the end, their combined Coryat score was $53,200: twenty-five right responses for Holzhauer, twenty-one for Boettcher, and thirteen for Sexton, plus that single wrong one. The trio added one final flourish to their almost-perfect game: Although

Final Jeopardy! is not included in Coryat scores, all three got the last question right. It was sixty-one up, sixty down—a singular feat in *Jeopardy!* history.

"At least if I'm going to lose," Sexton says, "I lost in a historic game."

—

WHAT WAS THE WORST GAME OF *JEOPARDY!* EVER?

A three-way tie for zero is, basically, the version of the prisoner's dilemma where everyone stays behind bars for the rest of their lives: All three contestants go home, but are forced to live in *Jeopardy!* infamy forevermore.

It's a rare *Jeopardy!* occurrence, but it does happen. According to *The Jeopardy! Fan*, it has happened just seven times in the show's history, three of which were during tournaments—situations where players might have been more inclined to bet everything in Final Jeopardy! than they otherwise would.

It's an outcome nearly as old as the show itself, with the first three-way zero coming in just the second episode of the Alex Trebek reboot, making for a curious farewell to the new version's very first champion, Greg Hopkins. The most recent example was in January 2016, when reigning champion Mike Drummond and opponent Claudia Corriere entered Final Jeopardy! tied for the lead with $13,800. Both bet everything and were wrong, as did (and was) third-place contender Randi Kristensen, meaning all three improbably bottomed out. Magnanimously, the show sent both Drummond and Corriere home with the $2,000 consolation prize usually reserved for second-place finishers. (As a further curiosity, Corriere had actually won two games a month earlier but been unable to return for her third episode due to a work conflict, so entered this game a co-champion.)

But while collective zilches are impressive, in the search for *Jeopardy!*'s worst game, I am partial to another form of ignominy: the October 17, 2017, game in which naval officer Manny Abell won with a single dollar.

Abell was actually the second *Jeopardy!* contestant to do this. In 1993, Darryl Scott entered Final Jeopardy! with a $1 lead over the returning champion, Nancy Melucci. Melucci bet it all, while Scott bet everything but a dollar; they, plus a distantly trailing Kate Marciniak in third place, all missed the Final Jeopardy! clue, and so Scott made off with a buck's worth of winnings.

But Abell's game was different. Where Scott entered Final Jeopardy! leading the pack, Abell—

then a two-day winner with $42,798 to his name, so certainly no slouch—did no such thing. He entered Final Jeopardy! with just $1,000 and his opponents, Fran Fried and Carlos Nobleza Posas, tied at a distant $12,300. His run, surely, was over.

Then they bet it all, and Abell bet $999, and it turns out that none of them had quite as strong a grasp of Asian geography as they had hoped. When the camera panned to Abell and the $1 now illuminated on his display, he could only shrug. The players he beat walked away with significantly higher paydays: Fried with $1,999 more than him and Nobleza Posas with $999.

If you consider the goal of *Jeopardy!* to be someone emerging with a clear-cut victory, a different kind of contender for "worst" emerges.

There has been a three-way, nonzero tie just once: On March 16, 2007, when Anders Martinson, Jamey Kirby, and defending champion Scott Weiss all finished with a total of $16,000. Because tiebreakers had not yet been instituted, all three were named co-champions, given their $16,000, and welcomed back to play a second game. (Kirby won.)

The tie was the handiwork of Weiss, who entered Final Jeopardy! with a commanding, albeit not runaway, lead: $13,400, while his opponents both had $8,000. Realizing they both might bet the farm, he threw a wrench into the Trebekatron and wagered $2,600 to match them. As Weiss suspected they would, Martinson and Kirby had indeed gone all in; all three players were right, and voilà.

"I thought it would be neat to share the money," Weiss, a longtime *Jeopardy!* viewer, wrote of the game later on his personal blog. Seeming to recognize the enduring weirdness that such a moment would offer, he added, "Now there'll be a notation next to one of my games in the J! Archive. How cool is that?"

Everyone walked away with a substantial payday, so you could perhaps argue that this was one of the best games in *Jeopardy!* history. At the very least, it was one of the strangest.

One scenario has not yet been put to the test. *Jeopardy!* policy holds that if all three players have negative scores or $0 after Double Jeopardy!, Final Jeopardy! will not be played. It has never happened—or at least not yet.

CHAPTER FIVE

WEIRD AL, TURD FERGUSON, AND CLIFF CLAVIN

JEOPARDY! IN POP CULTURE

In the department of alternate realities, here's one: Without Weird Al Yankovic, *Jeopardy!* might not exist today.

In 1983, *Jeopardy!* had functionally been off the air for eight years. The original version had been popular, but a decade in, NBC decided to move it to an earlier time slot. Ratings plummeted, and the quiz show—save a 1978–1979 revival as *The All-New Jeopardy!* with significant rule changes, to Merv Griffin's chagrin—seemed to be through.

Then, in early 1983, the Greg Kihn Band released "Jeopardy." The song was emphatically not about the erstwhile game show: "Our love's in jeopardy, baby, ooh," Kihn crooned through the chorus. It was a hit, climbing to no. 2 on the *Billboard* Hot 100 and catching the eye of a young parodist.

"I was a big fan of the game show *Jeopardy!* when I was a little kid in the '60s," Yankovic remembers. "And I just thought that that was a natural twist on the song, to give it more of a pop-culture bent."

Yankovic, who was in the process of building out his second album, *In 3-D*, intended the tune purely as a throwback: "a bit of nostalgia," as he puts it. "It was the old show hosted by Art Fleming, with Don Pardo as the announcer, which I honestly just had the vaguest memory of, but I thought, well, this would be a fun thing to write a song about."

And so, having secured Kihn's blessing, he did. The result, recorded in December 1983, was "I Lost on *Jeopardy*," a buoyant imagining of the plight of an overmatched contestant. "I was there to match my intellect on national TV," sang Yankovic, "against a plumber and an architect, both with a PhD." He picks "Potpourri" and finds a Daily Double—"and then my mind went blank."

Yankovic enlisted no less than the actual Fleming and Pardo, with Pardo—by then having moved on to announcing duties at *Saturday Night Live*—delivering a furious diatribe about the prizes Yankovic missed out on (encyclopedias, Rice-A-Roni) and concluding, "You brought shame and disgrace to your family name for generations to come."

Both originals participated in the music video, Pardo remotely from New York City and Fleming, Yankovic remembers to his enduring delight, turning up to the shoot "disco'd out—he had gold chains and was looking much hipper than you're used to Art Fleming looking on TV." Kihn appeared as well, driving the getaway car that Yankovic finds himself hurled into post-loss by burly studio hands.

Yankovic's version of "Jeopardy" was a hit, too, peaking at no. 81 on the Hot 100 in July 1984. And suddenly, everyone was talking about *Jeopardy!*

Unbeknownst to Yankovic, he wasn't the only one thinking about the good old days of *Jeopardy!* in 1983. So, too, was the show's creator. "We were experiencing tremendous success running a nighttime version of *Wheel of Fortune*," Griffin recalled in 1990's *The Jeopardy! Book*, "and wanted to try *Jeopardy!* in the evening markets."

Griffin was eager to experiment with *Wheel* in syndication, and he thought a *Jeopardy!* revival might pair well with it. In September 1983, King World, soon to become the revival's syndicator, test-marketed a pilot of a new version of *Jeopardy!* with Alex Trebek behind the lectern—three months before "I Lost on *Jeopardy*" was recorded. (*The Jeopardy! Book* was coauthored by Trebek and Peter Barsocchini, who a decade earlier had ghostwritten Griffin's autobiography. In 2004, Barsocchini would write a script for his young daughter and her friends: *High School Musical*. It did pretty well.)

But the 1983 Trebek pilot was a flop. It went unaired, and, as Griffin remembered, "the research came back lousy, indicating that viewers weren't interested in *Jeopardy!* returning to television." Griffin—who once joked to the *New York Times* that he hoped his tombstone would read "I will not be right back after these messages"—trudged forward anyway. Harry Eisenberg, a producer who worked on the first seven years of the new show, recalled getting a call from Trebek himself in March 1984 inviting him to an audition the following month, with prep for taping scheduled to begin in early June.

As it happened, "I Lost on *Jeopardy*" was released the very day that *Jeopardy!*'s newly hired staff first gathered at the show's new studio on Sunset Boulevard. The day after, the writers arrived to explore the show's freshly assembled research library, as Eisenberg remembered in 1995's *Jeopardy!: A Revealing Look Inside TV's Top Quiz Show*.

"One thing Jules [Minton, the revival's first head writer] made sure to do that first day was to play for us the popular video 'I Lost on *Jeopardy*' by 'Weird Al' Yankovic," Eisenberg wrote.

Eisenberg might have been happy to get the gig, but he didn't necessarily get what Yankovic was doing. "I was surprised 'I Lost on *Jeopardy*' was so popular," he continued. "It got ample air play even though the show hadn't been on in years. Maybe it was an omen of good things to come."

Griffin certainly thought so. In June 1984, with production of the revival ramping up ahead of the show's first season, Yankovic was invited on Griffin's talk show, *The Merv Griffin Show*, where he and his band delivered a gleeful performance of "I Lost on *Jeopardy*" in front of the studio audience. Then Griffin, who'd introduced Yankovic's song by declaring it "very close to [his] heart," joined the Hawaiian shirt–clad singer upstage.

No one ever accused Griffin of missing a promotional opportunity. "Al, Al, what you've done for me, I can't tell you," Griffin said to Yankovic. "With the great success of that record, *Jeopardy!*'s coming back in September of this year."

And so it did, premiering on September 10, 1984. The show was an immediate hit: The first season's ratings were so high that management issued staff a midseason $50-a-week raise, according to *A Revealing Look* (perhaps more an indication of the show's original shoestring budget). By the season's end, *Jeopardy!* ranked in the top five of all syndicated shows. In New York City, it was such a sensation that Dan Rather's evening news broadcast was moved up half an hour to avoid competing with it.

That a hit song about the show happened to dominate the radio in the months before its debut, filling listeners with Yankovic's "bit of nostalgia," surely couldn't have hurt. (It also probably didn't hurt that the board game Trivial Pursuit, originally released a few years earlier, had kicked off a full-blown nationwide trivia craze.)

Yankovic's song has continued to resonate in the *Jeopardy!*-verse in the nearly forty years since it was recorded. It's a one-and-done anthem, as well as one adopted by those who've lost in more illustrious ways. After he came in second in the Greatest of All Time tournament in 2020, James Holzhauer set his Twitter profile picture to an image of Yankovic in the "I Lost on *Jeopardy*" music video, the score on his podium marked 0. (Holzhauer, for what it's worth, *did* walk away with $250,000 for his loss.)

On *The Merv Griffin Show*, Griffin sent Yankovic off with a lament. "If I'd have just thought of it, you could have done the Art Fleming role on that show," he said, as the singer looked bashful. "Or Don Pardo."

Griffin was likely joking, always and forever the showman. But I ask Yankovic: What if he had been serious? What if, instead of the snappy, salt-and-pepper-haired Canadian, Griffin had asked Yankovic to host his show's revival?

"Oh gosh, did he say that?" Yankovic replies. "Oh wow, 1984 me is different than current me—my career was just starting out…" He trails off, seemingly wondering at this bizarre road not taken. "That's one of those hypothetical situations that's hard to answer at this point in time. But I would have had to really consider it, I guess."

Perhaps if things had shaken out a little differently, we might have spent the ensuing decades watching Weird Al deliver answers and questions, none the wiser to "Amish Paradise."

WHO IS KAREEM ABDUL-JABBAR?

"I want America," says Kareem Abdul-Jabbar, "to see that athletes are much more complex than just dumb jock stereotypes that we often see in movies."

The nineteen-time NBA All-Star is one of the most successful contestants in the history of *Celebrity Jeopardy!* He has appeared four times—1994, 1998, 2009, and 2012—twice winning and twice coming in second.

On *Jeopardy!*, he was not simply dominant. He was the kind of player who, when greeted with the Final Jeopardy! clue "He lived with his girlfriend, a fat priest & a 7-foot-tall archer" (a strong case for the Oxford comma), answered with the folk hero's formal name, Robin of Locksley. (The six-time MVP did offer the character's more famous nickname— "Robin Hood"—in a parenthetical.)

In response to being ruled incorrect on the clue "Of Norway, Sweden & Denmark, this one is the largest in area," he challenged Alex Trebek onstage, telling him, "If you include Greenland, which is part of Denmark, Denmark is the biggest." After a time-out, the judges agreed.

He also managed to do something no other contestant ever has—or, specifically, two things. During a 2009 game of the Million Dollar Celebrity Invitational, he rang in on the $400 clue under the category "I Went to UCLA"—his alma mater, coincidentally.

"You're gonna love it," said Trebek before reading the clue: "Tell your old man to drag this '70s UCLA & Trail Blazer center (& Lanier!) up & down the court for 48 minutes."

The clue was a reference to Abdul-Jabbar's cameo in the 1980 movie *Airplane!*, in which a child identifies the center despite his repeated insistence that he is a copilot named Roger Murdock. The boy is able to get the basketball great to break character by saying that his dad—a Lakers season ticket holder—doesn't believe Abdul-Jabbar works hard enough on defense or really tries—"except during the playoffs."

"The hell I don't!" Abdul-Jabbar snaps. "Listen, kid: I've been hearing that crap ever since I was at UCLA. I'm out there busting my buns every night! Tell your old man to drag Walton and Lanier up and down the court for 48 minutes!" (*Airplane II: The Sequel* would feature another cameo: Art Fleming.)

But on the *Jeopardy!* stage, Abdul-Jabbar forgot his line—and, apparently, the fact that he never played basketball for Portland. The clue referred to fellow UCLA alum Bill Walton.

And so Abdul-Jabbar became the first player in *Jeopardy!* history to guess himself as the answer to a clue—as well as the first to guess himself and be wrong. (The first part had *almost* happened a decade earlier, when anchor Robin Roberts correctly identified Phillies star Robin Roberts as the leader in a number of 1950s National League pitching statistics. "You don't look old enough to have set that record," said Trebek.)

"No!" cried Trebek (who, as a devoted Lakers fan, once said that Abdul-Jabbar would be first on his personal NBA Mount Rushmore).

"I thought it might be a trick question," remembers Abdul-Jabbar, "because it would be too easy for me to say myself. I kind of outsmarted myself."

Onstage, he clapped his hand to his mouth and laughed.

"That's another thing I like about the show. It can be very humbling," says Abdul-Jabbar.

"For me, it's like watching a professional sporting event," he adds of *Jeopardy!*'s appeal. "The audience doesn't think they could do as well, but the fact that somebody knows all that means it's possible."

It's what plays out endlessly on *Groundhog Day*, with Bill Murray's Phil gradually memorizing every single answer. It's what's on TV when one of the titular aliens bursts into a woman's home in *Predator 2*; in *Rain Man*, whose daily broadcasts Dustin Hoffman's Raymond uses to keep track of time; in *Mr. and Mrs. Smith,* what keeps an arms dealer's stooges distracted while Angelina Jolie's assassin does the job. In *Die Hard*, Bruce Willis's John McClane taunts villain Hans Gruber with a buzzer sound: "Sorry Hans, wrong guess. Would you like to go for Double Jeopardy! where the scores can really change?" (A "yippee-ki-yay" soon follows.)

Jeopardy!'s pop-culture omnipresence all started, according to Trebek, with *Cheers*.

In 1990, Trebek was asked to do a walk-on for the hit NBC comedy. "I went to the reading with the entire cast at the beginning of the week," he remembered in a break during the filming of the All-Star Games. "They discovered that, hey, Trebek can deliver lines. So the next day I showed up and there were more lines for me, and then the next day there were *more* lines. And then there was Cliff Clavin."

The resulting episode, "What Is…Cliff Clavin?," has become a classic—both of *Cheers* and of *Jeopardy!* It also kick-started a spree of '90s Trebek cameos.

He refereed a showdown between Bea Arthur's Dorothy and Betty White's Rose on *Golden Girls*, was rescued from the surf on *Baywatch*, denigrated a lousy GPA on *Beverly Hills, 90210*, and oversaw the victory of Rosie Perez's "former disco queen" Gloria over (no sweat) a teacher and a rocket scientist in *White Men Can't Jump*. In the span of one year, 1996, Trebek appeared on *The X-Files* (where he and Jesse Ventura tormented special agent Fox Mulder as mysterious men in black), *Seinfeld* (where he appeared in a not-actually-aired episode that George Costanza, suddenly celibate and just as suddenly brilliant, casually aces from home: "What is tungsten or wolfram?" quoth both Costanza and Trebek), and *The Magic School Bus* (where he, animated mustache and all, awarded Ms. Frizzle's kiddos "the Stanley Cup of show-and-tell-dom").

Naturally, the show is often used as proof of a character's smarts, as in the 2000 reboot of *Charlie's Angels*, whose opening credits show Cameron Diaz's brainy heroine being anointed a five-day champion with a total of $118,599—topping even Frank Spangenberg's then-record $102,597; "Way to go, Natalie!" Trebek exclaims. Even Taco Bell's Chihuahua mascot got a shot in an ad, firing off "what's a logarithm?" at the host while in pursuit of (what else?) a taco. More recently, Trebek turned up on *Orange Is the New Black*, where an inmate's television-themed hallucination results in Trebek—the patron saint of Canadian niceties, the apple of your grandmother's eye—delivering the following line: "I'm here, bitch."

ANDY RICHTER, THE KING OF CELEBRITY JEOPARDY!

No less than Alex Trebek declared the comedian Andy Richter perhaps the finest *Celebrity Jeopardy!* contestant in the show's history. Conan O'Brien's late-night sidekick has played twice, in 1999 and then again a decade later in an early round of the Million Dollar Celebrity Invitational, a pseudo—

Tournament of Champions for previous celebrity winners with a $1 million grand prize.

Richter won on both occasions, reaching a mark of $68,000 in his second appearance—not just the highest score in *Celebrity Jeopardy!* history, but also at the time a tie for the second-highest *Jeopardy!* score ever.

Richter is circumspect about the record, which he qualifies as having happened on "dum-dum pretty people *Jeopardy!*": "I would be a pretty good, *okay* regular *Jeopardy!* player," he says, "but I'm a really good celebrity player. They're not there to make the celebrities look like idiots, so they're going to tone it down a little bit."

Richter's record-setting game also featured a historic shellacking of opponent Wolf Blitzer.

"Everybody who was there had done well in previous *Celebrity Jeopardy!* appearances," Richter remembers of facing Blitzer and actress Dana Delany. "Wolf Blitzer—you know, I'm intimidated! He's a news guy. As much as he's a little stiff and seems a little square, it's like, well, he's gotta know stuff."

Instead, the CNN anchor faceplanted. "I don't know what happened," Richter says. "He just had lots of brain farts, I think—I hate that phrase but it's so descriptive. He said that Jesus was born in Jerusalem. He can't really think that—he probably kicked himself after that, like: No shit, Jesus was born in Bethlehem."

Blitzer finished Double Jeopardy! with a score of negative $4,600. To keep him in the game, the show changed his score to $1,000 for Final Jeopardy!—he got it right—but the damage was done. "It wasn't fun," says Richter. "Going into the green room afterward—his wife was there, and they just hightailed it out of there."

Ultimately, Richter bowed out of the tournament's semifinals: The game would have taped in early 2010, just as a nationwide tour with O'Brien—scheduled for supportive fans in the aftermath of the host's ouster from *The Tonight Show*—was getting under way. "I basically got to live the life of a touring musician for two and a half months," Richter says, noting that it led him to the immediate conclusion that he definitely could not be a touring musician: "I would be a terrible alcoholic and probably weigh 350 pounds." Actor Michael McKean ultimately won the tournament.

Richter credits his background in television both for helping him keep his cool under the lights and for something perhaps more important: his buzzer skills. "In acting you have to sometimes do what is called ADR, which is Automated Dialogue Replacement, and it's where you dub over your own lines if there's a problem with the sound," he says.

As on *Jeopardy!*, ADR requires participants to precisely time their action to a sound cue. Richter says he'd always had a knack for it, so when it came to *Jeopardy!*, he found he was able to box out the competition right away. During a commercial break in his first appearance, he tried to make light of it to opponent S. Epatha Merkerson. "She was just the sweetest, I just fell in love with her," he says, noting that afterward she sent him a *Pee-wee's Playhouse* Reba the Mail Lady action figure, still in its original packaging.

"I was saying, 'Yeah, the buzzer can be kind of tricky to get a hang of,'" Richter remembers—at which point actor Brian Dennehy, who would finish the game in second place, turned and said: "You don't seem to be having any fucking problems with it." (As luck would have it, five years later, Dennehy's daughter, Deirdre Basile, would make it on regular *Jeopardy!*—and find herself playing, and losing to, Ken Jennings.)

Celebrity contestants don't keep their winnings, sending them instead to a charity of their choosing; in 2009, Richter's $68,000 went to St. Jude Children's Hospital. (The charities selected by the nonwinners get $25,000, so Blitzer's selection—the American Cancer Society—had a rather better day than the newscaster.)

In the 1999 contest, Sony spiced things up for its VIPs by anointing them with gifts. Richter remembers griping with *The Daily Show* host Jon Stewart, a fellow contestant, about the grab bag of Sony merchandise they received.

"We were bitching to each other like fuckin' entitled babies. Like, 'This is retail price!'" says Richter. "I was such a dick about it that I looked up the camcorder that I got, and I'm like, this is actually a discontinued model! They're giving us the old models of stuff!" (It wasn't all bad: Richter says he also got a big-screen TV and his very first digital camera. Says McKean, who was also called in for a 1990s celebrity match, "I got a lot of really nice presents for my fiancée and her kids." On that occasion, he was called in as an alternate, and he didn't even end up having to play. "Everything worked out great," he says.)

Richter says that while he's not a *Jeopardy!* die-hard, it's something that's always on his DVR. "It's a very pure environment," he says. "Nothing intrudes on it. It's its own environment, it's its own rules. Fashion doesn't enter into it. It's never been jazzed up; it's never pandered to any sort of prurient, fleeting interest in some sexy trend. It's just about people answering questions."

Trebek jokes that one of his favorite cameos is one in which he doesn't actually appear. An early version of 2007's *The Bucket List* had Morgan Freeman's and Jack Nicholson's late-in-life conquests concluding in Culver City. There, Freeman's character finally got the chance to realize a lifelong goal by appearing on *Jeopardy!*—only to collapse on the set and die. The scene was filmed in the *Jeopardy!* studio with Trebek, but afterward, the ending was changed. Instead, Freeman's character died at home; Trebek's scene was left on the cutting room floor. (Perhaps not coincidentally, *The Bucket List* was directed by Rob Reiner, son of noted *Jeopardy!* fan Carl Reiner, who in 2020 told the *Guardian* that he and fellow comedian Mel Brooks, at ages ninety-seven and ninety-three, respectively, were still getting together every single weeknight to eat dinner while watching the quiz show. When the coronavirus pandemic disrupted the routine, Reiner and Brooks settled for a socially distant version—calling one another each night as *Jeopardy!* came on to watch and discuss over the phone.)

"When I first read *The Bucket List*, I had tears in my eyes—it was that moving a story," Trebek remembered of the initial script. But whatever disappointment he felt over being left out of the final cut, it was leavened by the fact that more than a decade on, he was still getting residual checks for his non-appearance.

Celebrities are often delighted to find themselves mentioned on *Jeopardy!*—a fact that the show is well aware of, often courting fandoms online after pop-culture clues emerge.

During Seasons 35 and 36 alone, there was joy from Gwen Stefani ("So rad!!" she wrote), Stephen Colbert ("What is the greatest honor of my television career?"), Dr. Phil ("how exciting!"), Meghan McCain ("One of the most exciting things ever"—perhaps all the more so because her father, the late senator John McCain, was a onetime champion on the Fleming version in 1965), and Mindy Kaling ("I just feel #blessed that I could be apart [*sic*] of this #JeopardyJames era"). As Lizzo put it on Instagram, "BITCH BITCH THIS AINT A DRILL IM A

@jeopardy QUESTION MAMAAAAAAAAAAAAAAAAA I MADE IT I LOVE YOU ALEX TREBEK."

Even Frank Sinatra was tickled when he got a mention. Trebek said that after Sinatra, himself a loyal *Jeopardy!* viewer, was the subject of a category, he wrote Trebek a letter to thank him. "You had a whole category about me on the show last night," it read. "I became a star."

THE *WHO WANTS TO BE A MILLIONAIRE* FEUD

Alex Trebek long enjoyed a playful mock-feud with *Wheel of Fortune* host Pat Sajak. "I would pick his natural blond hair out of his roots, I would beat him with a vowel, maybe a consonant or two, and then I'd run like the devil," he once joked of how they'd do in a fight. "C'mon, *Wheel of Fortune*—you know the alphabet, you're in!" he crowed during the taping of the All-Star Games. "All twenty-four letters—you're in!"

But when it came to Regis Philbin, the host seemed to take genuine umbrage.

In the summer of 1999, *Who Wants to Be a Millionaire* debuted on ABC. The game show, with its high-drama progression through multiple-choice questions that repeatedly required players to go double or nothing in search of the final $1 million prize, was a sensation, if not an outright phenomenon. It reshaped prime time—*prime time!*—and was widely credited with kicking off a boom of mega-popular reality TV, most notably *Survivor*, which premiered the following year. That first summer, it seemed that people everywhere were suddenly asking, "Is that your final answer?"

During a talk with journalism students at the University of Georgia in early 2000, Trebek hinted that he was less than impressed by the caliber of players on *Millionaire*, where the questions—just fifteen total if a contestant made it to the end, and they could have some help from "lifelines" along the way—were decidedly more everyman than those on *Jeopardy!* "You have to wonder about some of the contestants on that program," Trebek said, mimicking Philbin's voice and asking, "What's the usual color of Post-its?," followed by an exaggerated "Uhhhhhh."

Nor, apparently, did he think much of *Millionaire*'s host, noting that Philbin had twice appeared on *Celebrity Jeopardy!* "And he finished third both times," Trebek added. After his loss in the inaugural celeb tournament in 1992, Philbin had joked that his buzzer didn't work; Trebek later presented him with a bronzed buzzer on *Live with Regis & Kathie Lee*.

But there was no denying that *Millionaire* was a ratings smash: ABC would rake in more than $1 billion before the frenzy—with twenty-nine million viewers tuning in for each episode at its peak—subsided. Philbin, anointed "America's favorite television personality" by the menswear label Van Heusen, was granted his own line of Regis-branded shirts and ties. In 2000, the director of men's fashion at Saks Fifth Avenue credited Philbin and *Millionaire* with boosting sales of solid shirts and ties across the board. Trebek's official clothiers—Mr. Guy and later Perry Ellis—were, apparently, chopped liver. (He eventually became a free agent; in 2016, his stylist, Phil Wayne, told *Vanity Fair* that he lately preferred Armani. Following his death, Trebek's family donated 14 of the host's suits, 58 dress shirts, 300 neckties, 9 sport coats, and assorted belts and sweaters to the Doe Fund, a New York City–based nonprofit that provides career training and interview wardrobes to formerly unhoused and incarcerated men.)

Jeopardy! insisted it wasn't troubled. "People on our program aren't there for the money," Trebek said. "They're there for glory, to show off their intellectual prowess."

But while *Jeopardy!* has never marketed itself as a path to riches, its comparatively modest prizes—the record for one-day winnings when *Millionaire* premiered was $34,000, achieved by Jerome Vered in 1992—looked like small potatoes in comparison with the glitz and glamour on *Millionaire*.

Jeopardy! responded in November 2001 by

doubling the value of the clues on the board. A top-line clue in the first round would now be worth $200 instead of $100, a bottom-line clue in Double Jeopardy! became $2,000, from the original $1,000, and so on. The *New York Post* summed it up: *"Millionaire* Makes *Jeopardy!* Cough Up Prize Money."

(The change happened overnight, meaning that the players on the episode on Friday, November 23, played for half the clue value that those lucky few on Monday, November 26, did. The new era did not start with a bang: November 23's pre-doubling champ, Trevor Norris, won $16,001 that day, while the winner on November 26, Harold Skinner, managed only $7,700.)

But while *Millionaire* may have initially left the show playing catch-up, *Jeopardy!* won out in the end. *Millionaire*'s aggressive scheduling and wall-to-wall marketing meant that the show burned brightly—and quickly. Two years after its debut, the show was down to ten million viewers, and by spring 2002, ABC had seen enough and dropped *Millionaire* from prime time. Through a succession of formats and hosts, it never regained the spotlight.

Jeopardy!, meanwhile, carried on. "We're comfortable, like an old pair of shoes," Trebek said at the time. "We don't come on with a splash." (Don't tell that to Pam Mueller or the always immaculately be-suited Brad Rutter and Buzzy Cohen, who served as experts on the 2020 celebrity revival of *Who Wants to Be a Millionaire* with Jimmy Kimmel as host.)

Back in 2000, when *Who Wants to Be a Millionaire* was still soaring, Philbin asked Trebek to appear on the show's celebrity week. He declined, saying he was just too busy.

And then, of course, there's *Saturday Night Live*. On the *Jeopardy!* set, Trebek usually fielded questions from audience members in the pauses between games, while the champion was backstage hurriedly changing into a new outfit for the next "day." It was rare that a Q&A would go by without someone mustering up the courage to ask Trebek: Didn't Will Ferrell's impersonation bother him?

Beginning in 1996, Ferrell began hosting *SNL*'s recurring *Celebrity Jeopardy!* sketch. The segments, which quickly became a fan favorite, feature Ferrell as a no-nonsense, oft-aggrieved Trebek, who tries in vain to wring answers out of the incompetent celebrities who appear on his stage—most notably Darrell Hammond as Sean Connery and Norm Macdonald as Burt Reynolds (alias Turd Ferguson—"It's a funny name," Macdonald-as-Reynolds explains).

Ferrell's Trebek is a caricature of what the least charitable *Jeopardy!* viewers might see in the host: someone bored, condescending, even hostile toward the show's players.

You might get where Ferrell-as-Trebek is coming from, given what he has to put up with. One edition features the clue "This is the sound a doggy makes"—about the level of difficulty the *SNL* "celebrities" can handle. Only: They can't. Connery rings in to offer, "Moo."

"No," replies Ferrell.

"Well," says Connery, "that's the sound your mother made last night."

"Beautiful," Ferrell often says when Connery says something particularly crude. "Do you kiss your mother with that mouth?"

That sketch began in characteristic fashion. "Before we begin the Double Jeopardy! round, I'd like to ask our contestants once again to please refrain from using ethnic slurs," said Ferrell, before noting that Macdonald's Reynolds led with a whopping $14 while Hammond's Connery "has set a new *Jeopardy!* record with negative $230,000."

As it turns out, the real Trebek wasn't bothered at all. On the contrary: When the sketch was included in Ferrell's last episode as an *SNL* cast member in 2002, Trebek himself turned up to close it out. "And what a ride it has been," he said, joining Ferrell at his podium, before directing a jab at Hammond: "Back off, Connery—I don't have to take that from you."

So beloved is the *SNL* sendup at *Jeopardy!* HQ, in fact, that clips of it are included in the show's welcome video for visitors to the studio. When Trebek shaved off his mustache in 2001— a mid-tape-day whim about which he did not give producers a heads up—he quipped that he did it "to make it easier for Will Ferrell to do his impression of me on *Saturday Night Live*." (Ferrell, who has occasionally reprised the role when returning to *SNL* as host, has kept the mustache going.)

SNL's *Celebrity Jeopardy!* sketches were the brainchild of Macdonald. He lifted the idea from *Second City Television*, which had its own recurring game-show segments called *Half Wits* and *High-Q*, both starring Eugene Levy as "Alex Trebel." *High-Q* was a sendup of Trebek's very first spin as a quiz-show emcee, when he, then still with the CBC, moderated a high-school trivia competition called *Reach for the Top*. (Which is to say that yes—he was the subject of spoofs from the very beginning of his quizzing career.)

Levy, who wrote the sketches, played a "Trebel" that would be familiar to any *SNL* viewer. "If you've been with us for the past two weeks, you'll know that our contestants are all tied for the lead: all at zero," he said grimly to open one sketch. "No correct answers thus far—two weeks, nothing even remotely correct. But we're hoping to break that deadlock tonight." His contestants, however, generally had other ideas.

Macdonald loved the *SCTV* sketches, and, as he told Howard Stern in 2016, eventually asked for Levy's blessing to bring the idea to *SNL*. And so he did, reproducing the prickly, exasperated Trebek and the rotating stable of know-nothing players (frequently the celebrity host of the episode), and adding an antagonist in Hammond's Connery and a disinterested agent of chaos in his own portrayal of Reynolds.

"Sometimes people ask me who the funnier character is, Connery or Burt," Macdonald wrote on Twitter in honor of *SNL*'s fortieth-anniversary special in 2015. "The funniest character in *Celebrity Jeopardy!*, by far, is Alex Trebek as played by Will. Without Will's perfect take on Trebek, maddened by the outright hostility of Connery, the faraway uninterest of Burt, the sketch is nothing."

As for Trebek: He liked Ferrell's version but said that Levy's was his favorite. "Will Ferrell on *Saturday Night Live* is very cool and doesn't get too upset," Trebek said in 2020 on a podcast with comedian Paula Poundstone. Then he added, more than a little admiringly: "But Eugene Levy—he'd let it rip."

In 2014, *SNL* added a second *Jeopardy!*-inspired sketch:

Black Jeopardy! Created by writer Bryan Tucker and head writer Michael Che, *Black Jeopardy!* takes a decidedly different spin on the show. Riffing on *Jeopardy!*'s familiar contours and staid, bookish conservativism, *Black Jeopardy!* delivers a raucous version of the show hosted by Kenan Thompson—who introduced himself in the first sketch as "Alex Treblack," before clarifying, "Nah, I'm just playing, I'm Darnell Hayes."

Trebek he is not, overseeing collision after collision between the show's Black cast members and fish-out-of-water outsiders—often white guest hosts—to send up and celebrate Black culture. If Ferrell's Trebek can't wait to punch out and get away from his contestants, Thompson's Trebek—er, Hayes—is a cruise ship director eager to see where the voyage might take them.

When cast member Jay Pharoah's "Amir" rings in on the clue "Chase Bank says 'You have money, but you can't use it until tomorrow'" with the right answer—"What is *psssh,* you better give me my $17"—Thompson explodes with delight. "There you go!" he exclaims. "You know how I'm saying? You know how I'm saying? Who are *you* to try to keep *my* money?"

Contestants on the real *Jeopardy!* have occasionally made homages to the *SNL* sketches. In 2015, contestant Talia Lavin devoted her Final Jeopardy! response to it: "What is the love ballad of turd ferguson p.s. hi mom?" Trebek gamely read it in full.

"I'm really glad that *SNL* ended up doing spoofs, because *Jeopardy!*'s been around forever," says broadcaster Meredith Vieira, who took over as host of *Who Wants to Be a Millionaire* after Regis Philbin departed in 2002. "Every show has its hyped moments and then people sort of forget about it. I think that put it back on the map with the general public who might not have been watching all the time."

Lavin was not the first person to work in a reference to *SNL*—the writers themselves are fond of including it. Double Jeopardy! of one game in 2001 was composed entirely of categories that had previously appeared on *SNL*'s *Celebrity Jeopardy!*: "The Number After 2," "Rhymes with Dog," "Therapists." ("Not," clarified Trebek to ward off any Connery-inspired misreadings of category names, "'The Rapists.'")

That game also featured "Surprise Me, Trebek," which has become a real *Jeopardy!* standby, appearing in everything from the Million Dollar Celebrity Invitational to the 2020 Greatest of All Time tournament. Also seen in episodes: "States That Begin with Californ," "A Petit Dejeuner"—even "The Pen Is Mightier" and "An Album Cover," which really was about album covers.

Take it from this 2016 clue in a category devoted to *SNL*: "Norm Macdonald created 'Celeb. Jeo.!' to get his impression of this man on 'SNL' & yes, Turd Ferguson is a funny name." At this point, loving Turd Ferguson is simply *Jeopardy!* policy.

The same goes for *Black Jeopardy!* In 2018, Harry Friedman told journalist Dave Schilling about his delight in an oral history of the sketch. "I remember getting texts from people who had seen the East Coast feed," Friedman said of the sketch's debut, "and they said, 'Oh my God, you can't believe what *SNL* is doing with *Jeopardy!*'"

On April Fools' Day of 2010, Ferrell himself appeared on *Jeopardy!*, subbing in as host for Final Jeopardy! while donning his *SNL* Trebek costume. It wasn't just viewers at home who were surprised by his sudden, unexplained appearance (as well as those earlier in the episode of Pat Sajak, Jeff Probst, and Neil Patrick Harris)—so too were the day's contestants. Says Jessica Trudeau, who won the episode, "We had no idea of the celebrity 'appearances,' because not only were they not in [the] studio that day, they didn't even show us the video of Ferrell doing his bit. Just standard Alex reading the Final Jeopardy! clue, with no indication they would be changing it later."

JEOPARDY! MUSIC

You might recognize the *Jeopardy!* theme song, and you've probably been humming the famous "Think!" music since you were a kid.

As with so much of *Jeopardy!*-dom, Merv Griffin is the man behind the curtain. The show's creator, who began playing the piano when he was just four years old, was said to have bragged about composing the famous *Jeopardy!* theme song in the space of just ninety seconds—while seated at a piano that once belonged to Marlon Brando.

Griffin, who passed away in 2007, once estimated that the royalties for *Jeopardy!*'s music had earned him a staggering $70 million. His son, Tony—the namesake of the song, which Merv originally called "A Time for Tony" in his honor—declined to give a current count in a 2019 ABC documentary, but acknowledged it's since surpassed $80 million.

On the show, the music's core has remained true to Griffin's original over the years. But every decade or so, the *Jeopardy!* team hires musicians to give it a refresh—often in conjunction with a new credit sequence. (The most recent edition was recorded in 2021 by Bleeding Fingers Music.) Some versions are funkier than others: *Rock & Roll Jeopardy!* unleashed an electric guitar version that was later adopted by the teen and college tournaments. The 2020 College Championship featured a jaunty rendition that goes heavy on the snare drums—originally the lead-in to *Sports Jeopardy!*

Per the official *Jeopardy!* store, which sells a T-shirt emblazoned with them, the "Think!" music's words are as follows: "*Doo doo doo doo-doo doo doo doo / Doo doo doo doo doooooo da-dum da-da-da / Doo doo doo doo-doo doo doo doo / Dum da-dum da dum dum dum / Boomp boomp.*"

In the end, Weird Al Yankovic finally got his shot at *Jeopardy!*

In 1998, he appeared on *Rock & Roll Jeopardy!*, the short-lived musical version of the show on VH1, hosted by a just-before-*Survivor* Jeff Probst. In Yankovic's episode, he faced Harry Wayne Casey—aka KC of KC and the Sunshine Band—and Gary Dell'Abate, the *Howard Stern Show* producer more widely known as Baba Booey.

On *Rock & Roll Jeopardy!*, contestants received the same preparation that players on the normal version of the show do, complete with a warm-up round to familiarize themselves with the buzzers. Yankovic, it turned out, was something of a natural.

"I was *killing* it in rehearsals," Yankovic says, "to the point where one of the producers said, 'Look, Al, just step away for a while and let the other two have a chance at it.' But then when the actual show started, Gary Dell'Abate smeared me."

Smear he did. Dell'Abate finished with $10,300 to Yankovic's measly score of $673. Casey rounded out the group in third place with $50.

In other words, Yankovic lost on *Jeopardy!*, baby. The producers were prepared for this possibility and played him off, of course, with a serenade of his very own song as the credits rolled. In his 2011 memoir, Dell'Abate listed defeating Yankovic on *Rock & Roll Jeopardy!* as the fifth-most amazing thing he'd ever done, right after meeting Bill Clinton.

Yankovic says that once the game started, he just couldn't get the timing right to ring in. "As many *Jeopardy!* contestants will tell you," says Yankovic, "it's all about being able to ring in on the buzzer in time."

He acknowledges that his loss has given rise to some conspiracy theories—namely, that he threw the game in the hope of living out the lyrics to his song. But, he insists, "I wanted to win. I just couldn't buzz in on time."

Adds Yankovic with a laugh, "Maybe the producers had something to do with that, because they really just wanted to play 'I Lost on *Jeopardy*' on the show."

CHAPTER SIX

THE FORREST BOUNCE, GAME THEORY, AND TRUE DAILY DOUBLES, OH MY!

STRATEGY ON *JEOPARDY!*

Let's be clear about one thing: On *Jeopardy!*, there is no definitive recipe for success.

There have been very successful players who've prepared exhaustively for their tape days; there have also been very successful players who maybe didn't wing it, but also didn't necessarily rearrange their lives around taping. Likewise, many a brilliant trivia mind has arrived at the Alex Trebek stage after months of flash cards, buzzer and strategy drills, and simulated studio sessions and then come up short.

A large part of *Jeopardy!* is and always will be luck: whether categories you've mastered come up, or whether the ones that do are instead favorites of the person next to you—whose presence there, on that episode of that tape day of that season, involves quite a bit of luck, too. (Sometimes it's no one's lucky day: Pity the poor souls who played on February 23, 2005, who had a mind-boggling 24 triple stumpers over the course of the game's 61 clues and missed all three Daily Doubles to boot.) As we've discussed, getting on *Jeopardy!* is extraordinarily hard to do; of those who manage to do it, three-quarters lose their very first game. Perhaps the only thing more preposterous than going on *Jeopardy!* is going on and thinking you can win.

But—but!—there are some best practices, and some very smart people who've found a great deal of success deploying them. Some players have been much more successful on *Jeopardy!* than others, and many of them have done it again and again, episode after episode, tournament after tournament. *Jeopardy!* might turn heavily on luck, but it does not do so entirely.

So what does it take to win on *Jeopardy!*?

There are two major forms of strategy that come into play during a game of *Jeopardy!*: clue selection and wagering. Reasonable minds can and do differ, but we'll move through both.

CLUE SELECTION

If you've dipped more than a metatarsal into the *Jeopardy!* pool, you might be familiar with the strategy known as the Forrest Bounce. Named for 1986 Tournament of Champions winner Chuck Forrest, Forrest himself actually called it the *Rubin* Bounce after the law school classmate who first suggested it. Alas, to the victor go some $250,000 of tournament-boosted spoils, plus notoriety.

During his initial run, Forrest had great success ignoring

what remains perhaps the show's foremost unwritten rule: proceed in an orderly fashion through the categories, top to bottom. Instead, he jumped wildly between categories and dollar values—winning a then-record $72,800 during his initial streak and creating, thanks to the generations of future contestants who would attempt to emulate his success, perhaps the most well-known advanced *Jeopardy!* technique.

While the Forrest Bounce is usually considered a form of Daily Double hunting today, Forrest didn't think of it that way. He intended it purely as a way of throwing off opponents, who might be too flustered by the rapid-fire category switches to ring in promptly. "If your competitors let their minds wander as you select," he wrote in 1992's *Secrets of the Jeopardy! Champions*, "they may not even follow you at all." (Mark Lowenthal, a fellow champion and *Secrets'* coauthor, noted that he preferred the top-down standard—the better for accruing a hot streak.)

Though it's often thought of as a recent innovation, Forrest himself introduced it during just the second season of the Trebek revival—which is to say that it's almost as old as this version of the show itself. Arguably, it didn't go mainstream with either viewers or players until perhaps its most notable practitioner took the stage: Arthur Chu.

In 2014, Chu deployed the Forrest Bounce to win eleven games. Unlike Forrest, he explicitly saw this as a way of sussing out each game's three Daily Doubles. By hunting for them, Chu gave himself both offensive advantages—he had the chance to add a bunch of money to his score—*and* defensive advantages: He was robbing his opponents of the chance to do the same.

There are some general rules for Daily Double location.

Daily Doubles, one of which is located in the Jeopardy! round with the other two in Double Jeopardy!, are never found in the same category. And, most important, they are disproportionately found toward the bottom of the board. During Season 35, for example, the average Daily Double in Double Jeopardy! was located 3.56 clues down from the top of the board, according to J! Archive. A Daily Double hunter will, like any other player, attempt to get control of the board by answering a clue correctly. But while a traditional player might use this opportunity to start at the top of a new category or choose the next clue down in the one just answered, a player seeking a Daily Double is likely to choose a square more likely to be hiding the bonus, even if that means going straight for the $2,000 clue in a category that hasn't been started yet.

Chu's technique worked. In his first game, he finished with a total of $37,200 to his opponents' $200 and $0; seven of his twelve games were runaways. In the end, he finished with $297,200 in winnings, then the third-highest total in the show's history, and later added $100,000 with a second-place finish in that year's Tournament of Champions.

His high-octane embrace of the Forrest Bounce proved divisive almost immediately. Headlines asserted that he had somehow hacked or otherwise broken Jeopardy!; four wins in, the Washington Post went with "Arthur Chu: Mad Genius or Most Annoying Jeopardy! Contestant Ever?"

Traditionalists complain that bouncing around the board often obscures some hidden hint or joke embedded by the writers in the downward progression—robbing players of the intended signposts and of the writers' painstakingly presented wit. It also has the disorienting effect Forrest first intended on more than just a player's two onstage opponents. Pity those playing along at home, who may be confused in precisely the same way as those opponents and aren't even guaranteed a $1,000 booby prize for their trouble.

Chu was unapologetic, to say the least. "This is a one-time opportunity for me," he told the *Wall Street Journal*, "and I'm not going to give up the chance to win tens of thousands of dollars for the sake of the viewers at home."

Trebek modified his own routine to accommodate bouncers. During games, he could be seen writing on the lectern in front of him. He was not taking notes: Rather, he used a crayon (the better to avoid any sound that might be picked up by a microphone) to cross off each called clue.

In a particularly colorful interview with Howard Stern a year after Chu's run, Trebek said that it's one thing for a strong player to hunt for Daily Doubles. But Trebek had a word for those who disrupted the game that way and then didn't have the trivia goods to back it up: "dickweed."

Chu, for his part, tended to get them right: He found twenty-seven of the thirty-six available Daily Doubles during his original run on the show and was correct on all but eight of them.

MAN VERSUS MACHINE: IBM WATSON TAKES ON *JEOPARDY!*

In 2011, the computers won.

Okay, maybe just in a narrow sense. That was

the year that *Jeopardy!* trotted out its two winning-est champions, Brad Rutter and Ken Jennings, to face IBM's supercomputer, Watson, in a two-game match split over three episodes.

The idea came from the stalwart tech giant, which saw the game show as a peerless opportunity to demonstrate the potential of its new answer-fetching system, named for IBM founder Thomas J. Watson. In the words of the then-head of IBM Research, the company chose *Jeopardy!* for a simple reason: "People associate it with intelligence."

The event—whose $1 million grand prize was bankrolled by IBM—was heralded as the second coming of chess grandmaster Garry Kasparov's 1996 face-off with Deep Blue, an earlier IBM super-computer. As such, it was a media sensation, garnering a cover story in the *New York Times Magazine* headlined "Who Is Watson?" and push-ing *Jeopardy!* to its highest ratings since 2005—the last time Rutter and Jennings squared off.

The logistical hurdles were significant. At one point, IBM and *Jeopardy!* producers contemplated putting the physical mass of the machine's de facto data center on the *Wheel of Fortune* set next door (the tournament ultimately taped at IBM HQ), or projecting holograms over a pillar of fog to give Watson a face. IBM computer scientists spent years finessing the machine, which struggled mightily to master language generally and *Jeopardy!*'s punny inquisitiveness specifically. In early development, it made delightfully strange errors like referring to Malcolm X in a practice game as "Malcolm Ten."

Negotiations with *Jeopardy!* were contentious, according to *Final Jeopardy*, journalist Stephen Baker's account of the showdown. At one point, IBM suggested that *Jeopardy!*'s writers might—unconsciously or not—end up designing questions specifically designed to thwart Watson, which struggled with more abstract prompts. "We're not doing the Turing test!" team lead David Ferrucci exclaimed to colleagues.

This, of course, would have been a violation of *Jeopardy!*'s most sacred rule—questions must always be written impartially—not to mention a likely violation of the FCC regulations established after the 1950s quiz-show scandals. When IBM pushed the point in a meeting with Harry Friedman and supervising producer Rocky Schmidt, things grew so tense that *Jeopardy!* shortly sent word that it was rethinking participating at all.

Jeopardy! came around, but hurdles abounded. Originally, the producers had contemplated allowing Watson to buzz in electronically instead of using a physical button, given that the device lacked, well, limbs. Things changed when it became clear just how much of an advantage Watson's circuitry provided. Generally speaking, it took a human two hundred milliseconds to transmit a signal from the brain to a finger in order to buzz in. Watson, however, could do it in a tenth of that, according to Baker. The two parties settled on a mechanical "finger" built by IBM, which its engineers estimated would slow down the computer's response by eight milliseconds.

If you're running the math in your head, you might see the problem. As Watson entered crunch time, *Jeopardy!* granted IBM access to notable champions from years past, including nineteen-time winner David Madden, whose streak was second only to Ken Jennings's at the time.

Madden played two games against Watson. "They gave Watson superhuman buzzer timing to the point that it was next to impossible for anyone to catch up with it," he remembers. "The game was literally rigged from the start."

Jennings and Rutter later said that Watson's speed on the buzzer caused an additional problem: Both attempted to ring in earlier than they otherwise would have, likely sticking themselves with the quarter-second penalty given to early buzzers. (Doing away with the penalty for the human contestants was discussed early on, but the IBM team felt it would give them an unfair advantage.)

"It's like saying who's faster: Usain Bolt or a racecar?" Madden says.

Madden narrowly won both his games against the computer, but the problem to him was obvious. He suggests that IBM ought to have given Watson an average of different human champion speeds—that way, it would have been a fair fight, not to mention a better test of what the company purported to want to show: whether its computer could answer questions better than the most successful *Jeopardy!* contestants. As it was, with Rutter and Jennings given little chance to win buzzer battles, Madden minces no words: "It was the lowest moment in the show's history."

Perhaps most interesting of all on a strategic level is that Watson played an awful lot like James Holzhauer, the better part of a decade before Holzhauer would take the stage. In practice rounds, Watson tended to start with the $1,000 clue, not the $200 clue. Ignorant of any hints given by working through a category, Watson pursued something more important: Daily Doubles.

"Allowing one's opponents to find the DDs can lead to devastating consequences," the research team concluded in a paper afterward, "especially when playing against Grand Champions of the caliber of Ken Jennings and Brad Rutter."

Originally coded with a set of heuristics that dictated its wagering technique, Watson grew radically more aggressive once it was updated with data from millions of simulated *Jeopardy!* games. With that data in hand, Watson determined that in most scenarios, it made sense to bet everything it had, or close to it. Upon being told of this development, Ferrucci "turned pale as a sheet," according to one of the researchers Baker spoke with, "and said, 'You want to do what?'"

In the actual games against Rutter and Jennings, Watson stuck to its guns. The computer—which had been flipped to something called championship mode that specifically directed it to search for Daily Doubles—was an avid user of the Forrest Bounce. Spurred along by its ability to outbuzz its human opponents, the computer found all but one of the games' six Daily Doubles.

If the computer's bets weren't outrageous, that was mostly a reflection of the fact that it was quickly apparent that they didn't need to be. The games were routs: Watson finished game 1 with $35,734 to Rutter's $10,400 and Jennings's $4,800, and game 2 with $41,413 to their $11,200 and $19,200, respectively. The cumulative scores had Watson more than $50,000 ahead of Jennings, the runner-up.

Watson lives on, both in the real world—in recent years, IBM has deployed the system for health care research—and on *Jeopardy!* In the final game of the Watson showdown, Jennings wrote "I for one welcome our new computer overlords" on his Final Jeopardy! board, a riff on a quote from the 1977 film adaptation of H. G. Wells's "Empire of the Ants" (as well as a popular tribute on *The Simpsons*).

In a 2011 episode, *Jeopardy!* offered a salute,

naming a category "I, For One, Welcome" followed by "Our New Computer Overlords." Later that year, nine-day champion Jason Keller copied one of Watson's more notable clunkers, in which the supercomputer guessed, in the category "U.S. Cities," "What is Toronto?????" In his game, Keller did the same.

"If you can't be right," he said, "be funny, right?"

James Holzhauer heralded a still more aggressive style of play. Like Chu, he tended to make his initial selections from the higher-value clues, where the Daily Doubles tend to lurk. But while finding those Daily Doubles was a critical piece of his strategy, his progression across the board often was neither the traditional top-down vertical *nor* the Forrest Bounce–inspired scattershot. Instead, it was frequently lateral, beginning with the bottom row, pointing to another piece of his plan.

For Holzhauer, it wasn't enough just to beat his opponents to the Daily Doubles. He was after two other things. First: a lock game, ensuring that his streak would continue. And second: a very high score. In order to get to the absurdly high totals that defined his run—by the end of his streak, he owned twenty-one of the show's top twenty-five single-day records, with a high of $131,127 reached in his tenth game— he needed to have lots of money in the bank by the time he hit a Daily Double.

On *Jeopardy!*, the largest possible prize from a regular game is $566,400, which would require a single player to answer every clue correctly, hit all three Daily Doubles at the very end of each round, go all in with each, and then do the same in Final Jeopardy! The most important part of that is *at the very end of each round*, which matters because that is when the player would have the largest amount of money to gamble with. No player is ever *actually* going to hit $566,400, but Holzhauer was the first to play over an extended period of time like he might have been trying to. ("Please!" the show begs on its website in a post that mentions the maximum possible winnings. "Do not share this information with James Holzhauer.")

The first—but not the last. In 2020, Holzhauer returned to the *Jeopardy!* stage to face off against Ken Jennings and Brad Rutter in the Greatest of All Time tournament.

Both Jennings and Rutter began their *Jeopardy!* careers, in 2004 and 2000, respectively, with the top-down, one-category-at-a-time method that characterizes the "traditional" way of playing. Likewise, both have usually been much more cautious than Holzhauer in their betting. Like Holzhauer, Jennings found plenty of Daily Doubles during his initial streak, but he was significantly more conservative with them, betting an average of $3,265 on each through his first thirty-three games to Holzhauer's $8,984. This difference in style adds up quickly in aggregate: While Jennings won himself $159,299 on Daily Doubles in that window, Holzhauer earned more than quadruple that amount, $654,416.

As GOAT loomed, many observers wondered how Jennings and Rutter could possibly defeat Holzhauer. A player sticking to the classic pattern of clue selection would likely be doomed against someone moving laterally across the board. Even if the traditional player happened across Daily Doubles stashed higher on the board, they would be unlikely to have enough money to counter a new-school player: Two-thirds of the total clue value in either round of *Jeopardy!* sits in the bottom two rows.

At the taping of the 2019 All-Star Games, as the eighteen storied champs (including Jennings and Rutter, whose team would go on to win) went through the traditional warm-up game offered to all contestants, even those with numerous tournaments under their belts, a funny thing started to happen. Every time a player happened across a Daily Double, the fifteen champs waiting in the audience would form an impromptu cheering section, shouting one word over and over: "*True!*"

As in all *Jeopardy!*'s warm-up games, the stakes were low—the money wasn't real and players were being subbed in and out just as soon as the contestant coordinators were satisfied they had the hang of the buzzer—and so those onstage happily obliged, going for true Daily Double after true Daily Double after true Daily Double, to the delight of their watching peers. It was chaos *Jeopardy!*—reckless, alternately high-scoring and disastrous, and tons of fun. It would never happen in a real game: Even if one contestant insisted on betting everything at every opportunity, they surely wouldn't find themselves playing two other contestants who did the same thing.

Except that in the GOAT tournament, with its four double-game matches, it did happen. Of the twenty-four Daily Doubles that appeared during the tournament's run, the player who found each either went all in or maxed out above their score ($1,000 in the first round and $2,000 in Double Jeopardy!) all but once. And it wasn't just Holzhauer: Rutter and Jennings combined for eighteen of those twenty-four opportunities. (It was Jennings who made the lone smaller bet, wagering $5,000 of his $8,800 in Double Jeopardy! of the tournament's last game, which he entered with a commanding first-half lead—perhaps making him a little more wary of losing everything.)

Jennings, who won the tournament after ceding just a single match to Holzhauer, did so by successfully aping the newcomer's strategy. He did so with aplomb, beginning with match 1, when he found the first game's final Daily Double while trailing Holzhauer, $8,600 to $9,800; his decision to go all in allowed him to win the game in Final Jeopardy!

In one of the tournament's most shocking moments, he bet the entirety of his near-runaway $25,600 in Final Jeopardy! during the first half of match 3, all but ensuring his victory before the night's second game could even begin. ("Ken es el Hombre," Rutter wrote as his Final Jeopardy! response in the second half, before continuing, to the delight of fellow Philadelphia sporting faithful: "Eagles Super Bowl LII Champs.")

Afterward, Jennings was upfront about his strategy. "It's really just a credit to James, how much he's changed the game of *Jeopardy!*, that Brad and I both came in realizing we were going to have to play like him if we were going to have any hope of containing him," he told *Good Morning America*. "That's just how smart and demoralizing his strategy is. You've got to make those big bets even if it scares you, because he puts the fear of God into the other two contestants."

It's unclear, however, if Holzhauer's success on *Jeopardy!* will provoke a revolution. The lateral strategy is supremely effective in the hands of players like Holzhauer and Jennings, who have both the trivia arsenal to reliably answer the show's most difficult questions *and* the buzzer prowess to maintain control of the board and beat their opponents (or at least most of their opponents) to the higher-value clues.

But the problem with bulldozing your way across the bottom of the board is that it is *also* the quickest way to get yourself into a deep, perhaps insurmountable, monetary hole. While no one is likely to send henchmen after a player who finishes in the red, as Trebek's animated counterpart did to poor Marge Simpson, if you miss a couple of $2,000 clues or blow a significant Daily Double, you're likely in big trouble. Even Matt Amodio, whose style across his 38-game winning streak in 2021 closely resembled Holzhauer's in many ways, showed caution: While he almost always went all in after finding Daily Doubles in the first round, his bets tended to be much smaller during Double Jeopardy!

Buzzy Cohen, who originally won nine games in 2016, wonders if we might be seeing the dawn of a different, if related, revolution. "Maybe it's the aggressive *preparation* era. If you're in control of the game, you can win a lot of games. You don't have to win with $100,000.

"When I first appeared on the show, I was more like an old-school contestant, in that I was just someone who watched the show," Cohen says. "I feel like more and more now, people are actively trying to get on the show for a long time and preparing themselves for that and studying what other successful contestants have done. I think that information is maybe just starting to have been around long enough to bear fruit."

The collision of the ultra-prepared and what Cohen calls the "sofa players"—he includes himself in this category—might be part of what's fueling the sudden rise of so many dominant champions, like Amodio and 40-time champion

Amy Schneider, who shattered records just months apart. "It's sort of like if tennis went from being an amateur game to being a professional game but it didn't happen overnight, so each season there were two new players who were full-time training and everyone else was a club player," Cohen says. "We're at a point where it's not all pro, but there are a couple people that are preparing in a different way than everyone else."

WHAT'S IN A PRIZE?

When *Jeopardy!* relaunched in 1984, one of the big differences was that the players in second and third place no longer got to keep their winnings at the end of the game. This, producers felt—particularly Alex Trebek, who for the first three years of the revival was a dual host-producer—would lead to more competitive games. In the show's original version, contestants were often cautious with their winnings late in the game: Why would the person in second risk it all to go after the leader when they could just walk away with whatever they'd already accrued?

Bob Rubin, the show's first producer, remembered a player who appeared on the original *Jeopardy!* in 1967 with a specific goal in mind: He wanted to win enough money to buy an engagement ring. Per 1990's *The Jeopardy! Book*, "He won a sufficient amount for the ring midway through the game and kept his mouth shut from there on." (The book also noted that as of publishing, he and his bride-to-be had been married for twenty-three years.)

But while today's second- and third-place finishers walk away with $2,000 and $1,000, respectively, that wasn't always the case. In the early years of the revival, the runner-up was awarded a vacation, while third place received about $600 worth of physical prizes. All three contestants received some additional trophies courtesy of the show's sponsors, which were, as a rule, decidedly unglamorous. At the end of each episode, Johnny Gilbert would list the hodgepodge of items awaiting the trio, a small step up from the original *Jeopardy!*'s endless supply of Rice-A-Roni: lipstick, frozen shrimp, allergy pills, shampoo, Centrum multivitamins, industrial paint remover.

In *Prisoner of Trebekistan*, contestant Bob Harris's 2006 tale of his quartet of *Jeopardy!* appearances, Harris described the sudden, strange deluge of rewards that began showing up at his home a few months after he played. There were, among other things, a bathroom scale, a pair of toasters, maple syrup, cough syrup, chocolates, tomato juice, honey, Sweet'N Low, Bon Ami cleanser, and large quantities of Ex-Lax—what Harris called "lifetime supplies of products I wasn't sure what to do with." It was enough to make you yearn for the ceramic dalmatian long offered on *Wheel of Fortune*.

Okay, maybe not. For Harris's original five-game winning streak, he also received two Chevrolet Camaros—his-and-hers, the show assured him—not to mention $58,000 in winnings. (He sold the Camaros.)

This, too, was the norm: Before the five-day limit was lifted in 2003, undefeated champions also went home with new cars. Alan Bailey, a five-day winner in 2001, walked away with a Chevy Tahoe, which he drives to this day. In 2020, Bailey was a writer on the celebrity revival of *Who Wants to Be a Millionaire*, which filmed on the Sony studio lot. On an unusually empty day, Bailey was able to park his Tahoe directly in front of the *Jeopardy!* soundstage—"the very spot where it was conceived," he says.

While the cash was the real draw on *Jeopardy!*, even that was subject to some restrictions in the revival's early years. The take-home pot for normal gameplay was capped at $75,000 early on, then $100,000, then $200,000; if a player managed to win anything beyond that during their five-day run on the show, they could send the remainder to a charity of their choice. Frank Spangenberg, the 1990 champ who long held the five-day winnings record, won $102,597. He sent the $27,597 of spillover to the Gift of Love hospice in New York City—just enough, he discovered later, to cover a new sprinkler system, which the facility had learned just the day before that it would need.

Today's contestants, who have no limit on what they can earn, receive their winnings with California state tax removed, and must settle up the rest with the IRS. *Jeopardy!* winnings are treated as income, so what contestants owe depends on how much they earn in their off-screen lives. (Advantage: students.) In the end, many end up owing about half of their prize. That toll is especially hefty for those who have won big: After James Holzhauer won $2.46 million, CNBC theorized that he likely owed $1.2 million in taxes.

WAGERING

If *Jeopardy!* announced tomorrow that it would be doing away with cash prizes and henceforth doling out simple bragging rights instead, it's a fair bet that cancellation would follow in short order. Say what you will for the glory of nerdy sports, but the money is what makes things interesting.

Jeopardy! is a game where a contestant is all but certain to have to do some gambling, perhaps multiple times, in order to win. So central is the idea of risk that it is, of course, in the show's name: To do well, you must put yourself in jeopardy. (Merv Griffin credited this to network exec Ed Vane, who told him in an early pitch meeting, "I like what I see, but the game needs more jeopardies.")

To many aspiring *Jeopardy!* players, the centrality of Daily Double and Final Jeopardy! wagers, and the sometimes complicated math and game theory assumptions that under-pin success with either, is a terrifying notion.

Enter the patron saint of *Jeopardy!* wagering.

"Math skill and trivia skill don't always go hand in hand," says Keith Williams. "When you're up there under the lights, even if you're very good at math, basic addition and subtraction is almost impossible, especially when you're considering tens of thousands of dollars could be on the line."

Williams first played on *Jeopardy!* in 2003, when he, then a freshman at Middlebury, won the College Championship, walking away with $50,000 and the keys to a new Volvo. In the years that followed, he remained a steady presence in the *Jeopardy!* community online and twice returned to the show for reunion tournaments.

But it wasn't until 2013 that his *Jeopardy!* fame was really cemented. That year, a friend named Megan Hickey found out she was going to be on *Jeopardy!* and asked Williams for help figuring out the math behind wagering strategy. He dove in wholeheartedly—as a student, he had once taken a class on game theory and devoted his final project to testing his classmates on their Final Jeopardy! wagering skills, adding some quantitative certainty to what often feels like a purely subjective decision. He presented Hickey with a twenty-page document laying out the basics and then some. "It was way too long," he concedes, laughing.

In the end, Williams's advice (we'll get to that in a minute) didn't do much for Hickey—she found herself trailing in a lock game and settled for holding on to second place. But he thought there might be an audience for what he had done in turning math (scary) into a simple, or at least simple-*ish*, decision tree (less scary), and launched a website called The Final Wager.

There, Williams began to obsessively catalog each evening's Final Jeopardy! He recorded nightly videos in front of a whiteboard, scrawling out each player's score and what he thought they should bet, then watching in real time as they mostly did not do what he had retroactively advised. In 2015, he pored over J! Archive records and found that over the previous five seasons, the second-place contestant heading into Final Jeopardy! had wagered what he considered to be too much a whopping 46 percent of the time, frequently costing them the win.

To the soft-spoken, scholarly Williams, this was nothing short of an epidemic—one he hoped to wipe from the face of the earth with something bordering on religious fervor. When a player named Sarah McNitt began a six-game run in 2014 by wagering $4,000 in a Final Jeopardy! scenario that seemed to call for her to bet significantly more, Williams was apoplectic.

He posted a video with his brother and occasional costar Cory by his side, which mostly consisted of them hollering "what?!" at each other—a reaction that wasn't tempered when McNitt made the exact same bet in her second and third games, too.

In time, Williams found disciples—notably eleven-time champ Arthur Chu, who readily copped to following Williams's advice. So strict was Chu's adherence to Williams's system—at the time, Williams advised gunning for a tie with second place, which meant both top finishers would keep their prizes *and* play another game—that he recognized it as soon as Chu's streak began.

Jeopardy! got rid of ties in late 2014 and now forces a tiebreaker instead, a policy change that was not *not* because of the growing popularity of Williams's system. Ties, which had previously been quite rare (an official companion guide released in 2004 noted that there had been just forty-five co-champions in the first two decades of the show), were now suddenly a regular occurrence.

"So many people were taking advantage of this advice to tie that sometimes they were having two ties a week," Williams says. Given the drawbacks for *Jeopardy!*—the extra expense of paying two players and potentially flying them *both* back for additional tape days, plus the further reduction of the already-scant slots for new players each season—it wasn't a great shock that tiebreakers were introduced.

As for McNitt: She and Williams struck up a friendship after her *Jeopardy!* run. For April Fools' Day one year, she commissioned Cory and a host of notable champions, including Julia Collins and Ben Ingram, to write pieces for a website designed to look just like The Final Wager. McNitt's site's name: Just Wager 4,000.

Years later, McNitt's joke still haunts Williams. "Every time someone wagers $4,000, which is actually very frequent, I wonder," he says.

LOCK GAMES AND THE PLIGHT OF CLIFF CLAVIN

For many *Jeopardy!* contestants, the goal isn't simply to win, or even to win big: It's to get to a lock game. A lock game—also called a runaway— does often mean, yes, that the victor has raked in substantial dough. But it also means something more important: The winner will get to play another game.

On *Jeopardy!*, a win is worth even more than it seems. While random chance would dictate that each player in a game has a one-third chance of winning, that's not what actually happens. In 2017, Andy Saunders of *The Jeopardy! Fan* pored over more than a dozen seasons of the show and found that the defending champion won their next game 46.26 percent of the time. Extrapolated out, that meant that a *Jeopardy!* champ had on average a 4.58 percent chance of winning another four games—reaching the critical five-win threshold that guarantees a berth at the next Tournament of Champions. A victory thus also offered an awfully good shot at a *second* substantial payday—champions averaged a bit more than $20,000 per victory in that window—as well as a decent chance of still-higher payouts, given that the Tournament of Champions disburses $490,000 to fifteen contestants.

Lock games also offer one additional advantage: They make wagering in Final Jeopardy! very, very easy.

If you're leading after Double Jeopardy! in a lock game, all you have to do is stay out of reach of second place. You can even let your hair down and write a joke answer—you've earned it, and you're going to get to play again tomorrow no matter what.

(The king of joke answers might be the legendary Leonard Cooper, who found himself substantially leading—though technically not unassailable—at the end of the 2013 Teen Tournament and, when he couldn't quite get to Dwight Eisenhower in the last leg of the finals, offered this Final Jeopardy! response: "Some guy in Normandy. But I just won $75,000!") All you have to do to win, in short, is not screw up your Final Jeopardy! bet.

And so we come to the sorrowful tale of Cliff Clavin.

In a 1990 episode of the sitcom *Cheers*, mailman Cliff Clavin makes it onto a taping of *Jeopardy!* Once there, he finds a dream assortment of perfectly tailored categories that launch him, easy peasy, into Final Jeopardy! with a nearly $20,000 lead over either of his opponents. (And before *Jeopardy!* doubled the clue values, no less.) But then— audaciously, foolishly, heretically—he risks it all for the category "Movies." The clue appears: "Archibald Leach, Bernard Schwartz, and Lucille LeSueur." He draws a blank, sealing his fate and sending the lawyer at his side on to the next game instead.

"You bet it all!" Alex Trebek, who ranked this as one of his favorite cameos, cries, aghast. "Cliff, why would you do something like that?"

Clavin's incorrect answer—"Who are three people who've never been in my kitchen?"—has become a favorite *Jeopardy!*-ism. It has occasionally been used by actual contestants in Final Jeopardy!, including Elizabeth Williams in 2014 (clue: "In 1937 his sister said he had 'hats of every description' which he would use as a 'foundation of his next book'") and Carolyn Walsh in 2018 (clue: "Leodegrance, king of Cameliard, gave the newlyweds a piece of furniture on the marriage of this daughter").

In a 2005 game, the writers opted to design a board around the *Cheers* episode, naming the categories "Civil Servants," "Stamps from Around the World," "Mothers and Sons," "Beer," "Bar Trivia," and "Celibacy"—the same ones from Clavin's game. One of the "Beer" questions went so far as to name John Ratzenberger, the actor who played Clavin, asking which beer company he appeared in ads for. (That'd be Coors. The answers to Clavin's, Williams's, and Walsh's questions, respectively: The real names of Cary Grant, Tony Curtis, and Joan Crawford; Dr. Seuss; and Guinevere.)

Thanks to *Cheers*, misplaying a runaway and costing yourself the win is known as pulling a Clavin. It doesn't appear that any Clavins have actually been pulled by anyone other than the original: Says Saunders of *The Jeopardy! Fan*, "As best as I can tell, this has not happened in a game or a tournament with civilian contestants," though he notes that it could have happened in a celebrity tournament, when all strategic bets are generally off.

But Final Jeopardy! does still go awry on occasion.

Even Julia Collins ran into trouble when she mixed up the math in the eighth match of her twenty-game winning streak and bet $101 too much, putting her lock in danger; she nevertheless got the question right and won.

Not everyone is so lucky: In the second half of the 2003 Tournament of Champions finals, Brian Weikle—who held the one-day unadjusted winnings record before Ken Jennings—misread his own handwriting, mistaking a six for an eight. As a result, he bet $200 less than he should have on Final Jeopardy!, costing himself the victory—and nearly $200,000 of prize money.

The most notable snafu might belong to Michael Scott, who played during 2002's Kids Week at age eleven. He entered Final Jeopardy! in the lead with $10,800 to his opponents' second-place tie at $9,000. Realizing they might go all in, he knew he needed to have $18,001 if he were right. But as he was writing his wager, he mixed up the numbers and was told, he says, that he could not change his entry: $7,200, $1 shy of the breakaway. Sure enough, one of his opponents, David McIntyre, bet everything and was right, as was he—leaving them tied at $18,000 apiece.

"People in the audience started murmuring," remembers Scott. "Alex went over to talk to the judges. I wanted to crawl inside of a hole."

The game was settled by a nerve-racking

tiebreaker: an additional clue in a new category, "Literary Characters," with whoever managed to ring in first with the correct response being crowned champ. As luck would have it, Scott's mother had just made him start the Harry Potter series, and so he was able to beat his fellow tween to name Professor Dumbledore as the Hogwarts headmaster.

"When they gave us the okay to go see our parents in the stands, I took off running," says Scott of reaching his mother. "On TV, you can see her nearly in tears, saying something to me over and over again: 'I am so proud of you.'"

So, if not a universal $4,000, how should you wager on *Jeopardy!*?

Williams says that his first piece of advice is to have enough money going into Final Jeopardy! that you don't even have to worry about it. He's joking, of course—there probably aren't a lot of *Jeopardy!* players who start their games hoping they *don't* achieve a runaway. But there is something to it. Holzhauer, for example, is remembered as a savvy wagerer during his original stint on the show, but he was often working so that by the end of the game, he wouldn't need to be: His aggression during the Jeopardy! and Double Jeopardy! rounds and propensity for racking up high-value clues and Daily Doubles meant that he had a runaway score in all but four of his thirty-three games, one of which was his loss to Emma Boettcher.

"Most people," Williams concedes, "are not that lucky."

Contrary to how it appears on TV, players get a couple of minutes to figure out their Final Jeopardy! wagers, using a Sharpie and a slip of paper provided by the show's staff. (They do this after the category, but before the clue, has been revealed. Once the clue has been revealed, they get only the thirty seconds to answer that are shown on air.) For many, this might be the first time they've done math by hand since they were in school, and suffice it to say that those of us who've left manual arithmetic in the rearview have usually done so on purpose. But Williams counsels that most of the time, the guidance is pretty simple.

How a player should wager depends on their position entering Final Jeopardy! In most situations, the person in the lead should cover for second place—assume they'll bet everything they have and get it right, and bet so that if you're also right, you'll beat them by (at least) $1. If it's a close game, that means it will be a large wager. The person in third place also faces a relatively simple gamble: Most of the time, you should either bet everything, assuming you're in striking distance of your opponents, or bet nothing, with the assumption that the players in first and second place will both miss the question (and have made large enough bets to doom themselves).

Things are most complicated for the person in second. The general wisdom is to bet to cover third place. But from there, says Williams, "there are a bunch of mind games."

As in other scenarios involving imperfect information, a player is in the tricky position of trying to guess what the other person (or rather people) might do. Unlike many of those scenarios, a *Jeopardy!* player has something of a road map for what the other person is considering. Your average

Jeopardy! contestant is likely to be familiar with basic best wagering practices, and thus reasonably likely to follow them. For example, according to the J! Archive, of the 118 games during Season 35 where the leader entering Final Jeopardy! did not have a lock, that player bet to cover second place 111 times—94 percent of the time. The player in second could, therefore, try to surprise the leader, perhaps by betting nothing and hoping that the leader's answer was wrong. And it very well might be: The J! Archive also tells us that just 54.95 percent of Final Jeopardy! responses were correct in Season 35.

The best players are often those most likely to be predictable, for the simple reason that they know the best practices and are likely to adhere to them. Consider Final Jeopardy! of the episode that saw Boettcher defeat Holzhauer, in which his small wager spawned widespread suspicion that he might have thrown the game. Boettcher carried a narrow lead over Holzhauer—they had $26,600 and $23,400, respectively—with Jay Sexton in third at $11,000. Boettcher made a textbook-perfect bet: She assumed that Holzhauer might go all in, which would have brought his score to $46,800. If that happened, she would need to be beyond his reach with $46,801, so she wrote her wager accordingly: $20,201.

But Holzhauer didn't go all in. Sexton complicated the strategy: He too might go all in, so Holzhauer had to stay at least at $22,001. Holzhauer knew, surely, that his only chance of beating Boettcher was for her to get the question wrong, and she was exceedingly unlikely to have been in the 6 percent of Final Jeopardy! leaders to make such a small bet that she wouldn't cover him. Therefore, it didn't matter if Holzhauer bet big or small—victory depended entirely on Boettcher's knowledge, so all Holzhauer could do was make sure he didn't fall to third place if he got the question wrong himself.

That's precisely what he did, betting $1,399; Sexton, likely realizing that his only shot was if both his opponents bet big and lost, wagered $6,000, ensuring he would still have a sizable pot of money to top all-in or near-all-in bets by his opponents if they were both wrong. In the end, all three players were right, and Boettcher was crowned the new champion with $46,801.

This reliance on classic betting strategy can backfire, however. One of the better-known scenarios in Final Jeopardy! is the two-thirds rule: If the player in second has two-thirds or more of the leader's score, it often makes sense for them to make a very small bet, with the assumption that the player in first would make a large bet to cover them and—as so many contestants do—get Final Jeopardy! wrong. (The two-thirds rule may also have had a hand in Holzhauer's small bet: Had Boettcher been wrong, she would have dropped to $6,399, while Holzhauer would have been at either $24,799 or $22,001—enough for victory either way.)

But if the player in first suspects that their opponent might follow the traditional advice, they might deliberately attempt to throw them off by placing a small bet of their own, with the assumption that the person in second hasn't bet enough to catch them. So widely known is this counter-strategy that it was included in IBM Watson's internal rulebook.

Daily Doubles present the other source of *Jeopardy!* jeopardy, and for this, we once again have Merv Griffin to thank. "Since I'm a game player," Griffin wrote in the foreword of *The Jeopardy! Book*, "I try to stick with my instinct about what parts of a game appeal to me; for example I love horse racing, so I stirred into *Jeopardy!* the idea of a daily double. I had to fight the network to use the term *daily double* because they didn't like its gambling connotation."

The conventional wisdom holds that you should in most situations go all in if you find the Daily Double in the game's first round: If you're wrong, the hole is unlikely to be so deep that you can't hoist yourself back out by the second round, which is where two-thirds of the money is.

Six-time champ and 2015 Tournament of Champions winner Alex Jacob popularized the idea that it's usually worth doing that in Double Jeopardy!, too—at least if you're confident about the category. During his run, he boomeranged between true Daily Doubles when he liked the category and $100 bets when he did not. Chu, too, was known for his all-or-nothing approach, once finding a Daily Double and telling Trebek…"Five bucks"—the minimum for Daily Doubles. The host laughed; Chu promptly answered with an "I don't know," and moved on to raking in more money.

Contrary to how it appears on TV, contestants are given as long as they want to calculate their Daily Double wagers. But while players theoretically have limitless time to add up the remaining money on the board and riddle out how close their opponents might get—three-time contestant Alan Lin is known for elaborate midair counts as he sorts through his options on his fingers—they still contend with the host. If players took more than a few beats to state their wager, Trebek was known to verbally nudge them—after all, he needed to beat rush hour home.

"Alex Trebek will prompt you and goad you—he'll be like, 'Okay, come on, I need your wager,'" remembers Roger Craig.

"And he's an authority figure, right? So, many people comply with that. You really have to prepare yourself ahead of time to be like, 'I'm going to think about this.'"

If all this sounds like a lot, you're not alone.

When we spoke by phone, one day before his flight from New York to Los Angeles to tape, it had been four and a half weeks since Kris Sunderic got the call and started his studying regimen—not that he was counting. (Okay, he might have been counting.)

By that point, he was feeling a kind of peace with his prep, if also maybe a little horror at how simply he'd once viewed things. This was especially the case with wagering; his plans for after we hung up, he told me, were to spend the afternoon doing math by hand, the way he would have to onstage.

"Honestly, I've learned so much about the game in the last month," he said. "I didn't know what a Coryat score was when I got the call. I didn't know what shortegy was, what Stratton's dilemma was"—two wagering scenarios that are sufficiently inside baseball that the message board JBoard contains a post wondering, "For example, would a player that knew I studied J! Archive betting strategies be more likely to use shortegy against me?"

"I used to think that people just bet on how confident they were on the category," said Sunderic. "But no, there is a way to wager to maximize the probability of winning."

Well, sort of. Days later, he found himself called up from the audience for the morning's second game. Thanks in large part to going all in on a Daily Double early in Double Jeopardy! and getting it wrong, Sunderic found himself in third place entering Final Jeopardy!: $9,600, versus reigning champion Sid Katz, who led with $16,600, and Nicole Economou, who sat at $9,800.

It was what's called a crush game—the second-place player (as well as Sunderic, in this case) was trailing enough that she would have to bet everything, or close to it, *and* count on Katz getting it wrong. Sunderic's only chance, he knew, was to go big and hope for the best, and so he did, wagering $7,001— enough to beat Katz by a dollar if he bet nothing.

Trebek came to him, and yes, he got it: It was China that enacted the "one country, two systems" policy. Then Trebek went to Economou, who had *also* bet to beat Katz by a dollar but got the question wrong, and then to Katz, who had bet enough to cover Economou if she were right but missed the question, too. And then, suddenly: *Kris Sunderic— champion—$16,601.*

Sunderic looked thunderstruck. His jaw dropped, literally, like in a cartoon. He grabbed his head, then clapped his hands to his mouth, laughing, breathing, gasping. Trebek came to shake his hand and congratulate him, and asked, "Are you hyperventilating?"

Then he said: "Well, you better pull yourself together because you have to be back out here in ten minutes!"

CHAPTER SEVEN

THE ALUMNI NETWORK

On a Wednesday night in Santa Monica, California, a funny thing happens. At an otherwise nondescript Irish pub called O'Brien's, a *Jeopardy!* champion arrives. Then another. Then another.

Here a Tournament of Champions winner. There an Ultimate Tournament of Champions finalist. There's Jackie Fuchs, four-time champion and former member of the Runaways. Raj Dhuwalia, hailed by no less than Ken Jennings as having an even finer trivia mind than his own. Dileep Rao, one-time champ and big-screen star. (You might know him as the chemist in *Inception*.) There: a three-time winner, half a dozen one-and-doners, and, oh yeah, all-time winnings leader Brad Rutter.

They've come for the world-famous (okay, *trivia*-world-famous) weekly pub quiz—widely considered perhaps the finest, and hardest, bar trivia anywhere. Since 2006, when Jerome Vered—a five-time champ back in 1990 and second runner-up in 2005's Ultimate Tournament of Champions—first stumbled across the quiz and started bringing along friends, it has become a magnet for *Jeopardy!* alumni in LA, and a pilgrimage site for those visiting from afar. "People plan their whole visits around it," one regular tells me knowingly.

Vered doesn't live nearby these days; many Wednesdays, Los Angeles traffic makes the commute ninety minutes or more. But week in and week out, he's there all the same, competing for the right to wear the ceremonial O'Brien's fez bestowed for unknown reasons upon the winning team along with a small cash prize. "You realize I could be halfway to San Diego now," he says drily, "but here I am in Santa Monica."

Not everyone who frequents O'Brien's has been on *Jeopardy!*, but most of those who haven't seem to be working on it. The night I visit, one regular has just taped an episode the day before (possibly the first of many, though she is sphinxlike on the subject) and has a line of well-wishers waiting to congratulate her; another player is set to tape the following week.

Mark May, an IBM program manager who has organized the O'Brien's quiz for two decades, introduces himself by saying that he has not been on *Jeopardy!*, but, having been tapped for an audition not long before we spoke, *is* in the contestant pool—for the third time. Once, says Vered, his team of *Jeopardy!* alumni made their team name the sum total of their show winnings—a high number, given that Vered alone has won just shy of $500,000. (This flourish ruffled some feathers, he concedes.)

Another time, Pam Mueller (winner of the 2000 College Championship) and Ken Basin (a 2003 College Championship semifinalist) wrote a category composed entirely of the clues that had stumped the *Jeopardy!* champions in attendance—usually ones that had cost them dearly, like Daily Doubles or Final Jeopardy!s gone horribly wrong, and whose answers invariably haunted them years later. (The once-stumped, now-haunted players were not allowed to help their teams on "their" questions.)

This is an auspicious night at O'Brien's: It's the second night of the *Jeopardy!* Greatest of All Time tournament. While this was appointment viewing for *Jeopardy!* faithful everywhere, it was especially the case here, where Rutter—favored by many a fan as the contest's favorite—attends the quiz most weeks. The GOAT episode was played live with the sound cranked all the way up; when Rutter arrived shortly before it began, the whole bar burst into applause.

Rutter, who'd taped the tournament a month earlier, watched diffidently as Ken Jennings and James Holzhauer beat him to the buzzer over and over. His compatriots were not so calm, getting louder and louder with each of Rutter's correct answers, groaning when he missed a Daily Double, and openly jeering when a question looking for Willy Wonka's iconic three-word farewell was met with a triple stumper. ("Good day, sir!" much of the bar shouted.)

Rutter lost, and badly—in the second half, he finished Double Jeopardy! with a negative score, meaning he was ingloriously booted from the stage as his two opponents answered Final Jeopardy! on their own. A sense of relief permeates the air when it's finally time for the main event.

My team for the evening is made up of a cast of O'Brien's regulars: Mueller, 2017 Tournament of Champions winner Buzzy Cohen and runner-up Alan Lin, and Dan McCarthy, who tells me he hasn't been on *Jeopardy!*—yet. (He *did* win $35,000 playing on the short-lived *500 Questions* in 2015.) The bar is packed, with clusters of trivia fiends huddled around every table in the joint—so busy, in fact, that the kitchen is overwhelmed and stops taking orders. (One weekly player, someone notes sadly, is on a months-long quest to try every item on the menu.)

Rutter seems not to have taken the evening's GOAT outcome too badly: His table adopts the team name "Not Around for Final Jeopardy!" for the night.

As a rule, *Jeopardy!* alumni stick together. While relatively few will be asked to return for reunion tournaments, nearly all will spend years—very possibly the rest of their lives—telling people that no, contestants are not given a study guide, and yes, the buzzer really is that important, and, well, they only got about ninety seconds total with Alex Trebek.

To unite those who have had this particularly nerdy blast of fame, players have organized on social media. On Facebook, there is an invite-only group for contestants with membership well into the thousands, plus myriad splinter groups: one for female contestants, one for contestants who want to talk about politics (discussions got a little too heated for the general population), one for those interested in crafting, ones for *Jeopardy!* parents and lawyers and librarians and teachers, and so on. Many find themselves still in touch with the cohort of players from their tape day, with the memories of those adrenaline-fueled hours in the green room—where senior contestant coordinator Glenn Kagan was long known to perform magic tricks between rounds of a Jenga variant called Tumbling Tower—still vivid years later.

And some keep doing what brought them together in the

first place: duking it out in trivia, either at conferences like Trivia Nationals or at places like O'Brien's.

Our team gets off to an inauspicious start, no thanks to yours truly. I fancy myself a perfectly decent player at my own neighborhood bar's regular trivia night, but I'm no match for the questions here. Writing the quiz at O'Brien's is considered an honor, and the duty rotates among the cast of regulars; tonight's quiz is the work of Cliff Galiher (2007 College Champion and Tournament of Champions second runner-up) and Hans von Walter (2010 College Championship second runner-up and an alum of *Wheel of Fortune* and *Who Wants to Be a Millionaire*).

Many of their questions sail straight over my head: "What athlete appeared in the five performances of the Broadway musical *Buck White* in 1969?" "What is the literary question, originally unanswered, that prompted the author to offer the subsequent solution 'Because it can produce a few notes, tho they are very flat; and it is nevar put with the wrong end in front!'?" "What relationship do Supreme Court justices Salmon P. Chase and Samuel Chase have to impeachment?"

(The answers: Muhammad Ali; Lewis Carroll attempted to answer his Mad Hatter's inquiry: "Why is a raven like a writing desk?"—*raven* being *nevar* backward; Salmon presided over Andrew Johnson's impeachment, while Samuel is the only Supreme Court justice to be impeached to date.)

On others, I've only just begun to grasp what the prompt is looking for when I realize Lin has already bolted off to hand in the answer. I've been informed by several people, in what they surely thought was a reassuring way, that all you have to do to be a real O'Brien's player is offer up a single right answer to your team. So far, I've got nothing. One question asks for the name of the smaller fictional forest, introduced in 1926, for which England's Ashdown Forest is the namesake, and I confidently suggest—*duh*—Sherwood Forest.

"Mmm," says Cohen, halfway through writing the correct answer, the Hundred Acre Wood, "I *think* that might have been earlier." He uses the same soothing tone you might with a child who's handed you a portrait of the family drawn in fluorescent green. Maybe on toilet paper.

In the end, I help on exactly two clues: identifying Topeka, Kansas, as the state capital that has twice changed its name to promote a certain Nintendo game (I once wrote a story about the US rollout of Pokémon in 1998, which saw tiny yellow plushies rain down on the rebranded "Topikachu") and naming brussels sprouts as a vegetable derived from the same species as broccoli and kale, prompting a fist bump from a probably-too-pleased Cohen.

It pays, it turns out, to hang with the kids in the know. At the halfway point, we sit in fourth place, but manage to pull into the lead by half a point at the close of the quiz. Tight margins are decided by tiebreakers, so we and the teams in second and third square off on one last question: List as many of the cats in T. S. Eliot's *Old Possum's Book of*—groans ring out as von Walter finishes reading—*Practical Cats* as we can in two minutes. (The O'Brien's quiz doesn't take itself *too* seriously.) Lin and Mueller are both familiar with the musical adaptation of Eliot's work, *Cats*—then in theaters in its bonkers cinematic edition, botched CGI and all—and, having named eleven cats, we walk away with the grand prize. A member of one of the fallen teams comes up to tell us that he hates either cats or *Cats*, or perhaps both.

"If it's your first time, you *have* to wear the fez," Cohen tells me. Red, lumpy, and best not inspected very closely, the O'Brien's winners' fez is stuffed over my head, and for the minute or two that I wear it, I feel, however briefly, like a champion.

For my measly contributions, and despite my protests that the actual brains of our operation should keep the spoils, I'm awarded an even share of the night's prize pool, walking away with three crisp five-dollar bills and the vague feeling that I've copied off someone's homework.

But I'll take it. Fifteen bucks for two right answers—it's not six figures for a twenty-two-minute game-show taping, but it's a start.

HOW DO YOU SPEND YOUR WINNINGS?

As you might expect, the sort of very reasonable person who makes it onto *Jeopardy!* often does very reasonable things with the proceeds: tuition and student loan payments, down payments, a no-nonsense car, an—*ugh, Mom, you're killing me*—IRA. Maybe, if they're feeling wild, a one-week tour of a European capital.

But while plenty of *Jeopardy!* champions have stayed where they are—after taxes are accounted for, precious few emerge with what is classically referred to as "fuck you money"—that's not always the case. Many a high-roller has used their payday to refashion their lives, leaving the drudgery of their day jobs behind to embark on a new, perhaps nine-to-five-less chapter. (That is, once their checks have finally arrived—usually a few months after their last episode has aired.)

Tom Nissley, an eight-time champion and runner-up in the 2011 Tournament of Champions, left his job at Amazon (he stayed, he says, "just long enough that they thought I wasn't going to quit"), wrote a book, and then bought his neighborhood bookstore in Seattle, Washington. He remembers sitting in the airport after his winning streak and being suddenly overcome by a mix of terror and sadness. "I think it was the washing out of the adrenaline," he says, "or just knowing that my life was about to change."

A number of *Jeopardy!* alumni's new chapters, perhaps unsurprisingly, have to do with trivia. David Madden was a twenty-three-year-old grad student when he first played, and as he left the studio after his twentieth game with vouchers totaling more than $430,000, he wasn't sure what he wanted to do. "I didn't have a specific thing that I had my heart set on spending the money on," says Madden. "It was more just: Whoa, now I can just sort of live and not worry about money as much." A quiz bowl alum, he ultimately used his winnings as seed money to found International Academic Competitions, which hosts, among other things, the annual National History Bee and Bowl.

But there are plenty of champs who embark on more colorful missions. Some use their dough to pursue off-the-beaten-path passions: Bruce Seymour, who picked up more than $300,000 after winning 1990's *Super Jeopardy!* tournament, refurbished the decaying tombstone of the eighteenth-century globetrotting performer Lola Montez, about whom he also wrote a book. And some have used their *Jeopardy!* payday to jump-start their careers: Future *Mad Men* creator Matthew Weiner used the $3,799 he won in a 1992 episode to help finance his first feature film. (He has joked that it was the only money he made during the first five years of his marriage.)

Then there's Marvin Shinkman, who fell in the finals of the 1986 Tournament of Champions to Chuck Forrest (of the Forrest Bounce). Shinkman, a professional stamp dealer whose son Ron would later win one game in 2001, had a very specific plan for his winnings. "I think I'll lock myself in a vault with a large box of stamps," he told Alex Trebek, "take off all of my clothes, and roll around in 'em."

If you had any doubt about Marcia Chami's commitment to the House of Trebek, just take a look at her purse, from which *The Jeopardy! Book of Answers* is poking out. She's been a loyal viewer since the very beginning of the Trebek era, she says: "I have watched *Jeopardy!* more than half my life." Which is to say: Don't ever call her at 7:00 p.m.

On this night, she's arrived at a warehouse just off the Las Vegas Strip with a couple of friends, intent on seeing James Holzhauer in the flesh. One night after Rutter hosted a watch party in LA, it's Holzhauer's turn. His name dominates a genuine Vegas marquee outside, blinking lights and all: JEOPARDY THE GREATEST OF ALL TIME WITH JAMES HOLZHAUER.

Inside, throngs of game-show fans young and old—some *very* old, and wondering, ma'am, if you're going to use that seat behind you or just keep blocking it—have questions. What makes Holzhauer so good? That Jennings guy—what's his deal, anyway? (This was solidly a home crowd.) Does Holzhauer want to host *Jeopardy!* someday? And will he sign Chami's *Book of Answers*?

Chami is a lifelong Las Vegan. She was a dealer at Caesars for many years—her husband is a poker player, and she says he approves of Holzhauer's all-in form—and her affection for Holzhauer was immediate. "He was so sharp and focused," she says—plus, perhaps even better: "He was a Vegas boy."

Holzhauer grew up in Naperville, Illinois, but moved to Las Vegas as an adult. He and his wife, Melissa, have embraced their new home: In the year following James's *Jeopardy!* run, the Holzhauers donated some $300,000 to charitable causes, principally in the Las Vegas area, from the Clark County library system to a local high school in need of new athletic facilities—a philanthropic project they eventually convinced the newly resettled Raiders to join. The watch party benefits a local charity that provides resources to homeless students in the area.

In the midst of his winning streak, Holzhauer was presented with a key to the Las Vegas Strip, and May 2, 2019, was proclaimed James Holzhauer Day throughout Clark County.

Apparel for the NHL's Golden Knights, who play just a few minutes down the road and whose in-arena host is on hand to shepherd the Holzhauers through a Q&A, dots the room.

Nineteen-year-old Sammi Farr is a recent *Jeopardy!* convert: It wasn't until the local news started hyping Holzhauer's impending appearance in early 2019 that she began tuning in. During his streak, she became near fanatical. "I was nervous every night watching," she says. "Like: Is he going to lose? Is he going to lose?"

When he finally did, she kept watching, and so in the months since, she's started building up her *Jeopardy!* bona fides. Her mom got her a long-sleeve *Jeopardy!* shirt for her birthday—she's wearing it—and a *Jeopardy!* calendar for Christmas.

As the evening's GOAT game gets under way, the Holzhauers settle into two seats in the audience; when James rubs Melissa's back, the fans behind them wonder if it might be a hint that things will go his way. They, alas, do not: Jennings wins his second match of the tournament, putting him just one night away from his eventual victory. "What*ever*," hisses someone in the crowd when Jennings pulls off a tough answer.

The night concludes with a long photo line. Chami needn't have worried about her book: Holzhauer signs anything and everything, including a stack of low-res, high-gloss photos of himself that one attendee in a large floppy hat happily announces that he printed himself.

He tells me that he had Holzhauer inscribe his "To Mr. Magic," and I will go to my grave regretting not asking any further questions.

JEOPARDY! ROMANCE

Perhaps *Jeopardy!*, with an ambience that falls somewhere between the SATs and a TSA security line, does not strike you as a place rife with romance.

Friend, you are mistaken: Michael Pascuzzi, the contestant who proposed to his now-wife, Maria Shafer, with a little urging from contestant coordinator Corina Nusu, was far from alone in feeling the love.

Over the years, *Jeopardy!* has spawned a number of loving relationships—some even between opponents. Stacy and Emily Cloyd met in the green room while waiting to tape their respective episodes in 2010, and then ended up playing each other—Stacy won with a lock game—and wed two years later. Catherine Whitten and Justin Hofstetter met on the bus to the studio for the 2012 Teachers Tournament; they welcomed a baby boy the following year, and married on the third anniversary of their taping. Maryanne Lewell and Michael Townes met at the Teachers Tournament one year after Whitten and Hofstetter, and eventually welcomed five of their fellow tournament alumni to their wedding. Brigid Laurie and Mark Urciuolo met in the 1997 College Tournament and now joke about *Jeopardy!*'s "Nerd Breeding Program." (They have two kids.)

Lincoln Hamilton first met Danielle Stillman when

he grabbed the seat next to her at their audition; after both had made it to the show, they became friends—and later more—through the *Jeopardy!* alumni Facebook group. Eddie Timanus, who became *Jeopardy!*'s first blind contestant when he cruised through five games in 1999, met his wife, a teacher, when she asked him for help incorporating game shows into her social studies curriculum.

Perhaps unsurprisingly, the Teen Tournament is often rife with young love. Laura Ansley, a 2006 quarterfinalist, went to prom with a member of her cohort. Emily LaMonica, a semifinalist in the 2016 contest, says that she asked Alex Trebek to her own prom; sadly for those of us hoping for a ruffled tuxedo shirt, he declined.

Sharon Gerber (née Druck) dated a fellow Teen Tournament contestant for two years after competing. That year—1997—the board broke down on the first day of taping. "It delayed shooting a full day," says Gerber, "which was probably hell for production but was pretty much a *Breakfast Club* situation for a lot of us."

In 2005, 1998 Tournament of Champions winner Dan Melia married his fiancée, Dara Hellman, on the *Jeopardy!* set in a ceremony presided over by four-time contestant (and 1998 Tournament of Champions second runner-up) Bob Harris. Vows were delivered by ringing in on a nuptial-themed board. (To the clue "A man customarily says this if he should consent to have this woman to [be] his wedded wife": "What is 'I do'?, Bob," said Melia as Hellman beamed at his side.)

Trebek, who watched from the most unfamiliar vantage of the audience, served as the official witness.

Then there's the *Jeopardy!* staff. The book *This Is Jeopardy!* noted in 2004 that there have been no fewer than four marriages between *Jeopardy!* staff members over the years.

Kristin Sausville was a third of the way through taping *Jeopardy!* when she knew she needed to quit.

Yes, she'd wanted to go on the venerable quiz show for years, and yes, she'd spent months preparing, and yes, she had already paid for her flights and her Culver City hotel and made her way that morning in 2015 to the Sony Pictures studio lot. But there under the lights of the stage she'd dreamed of for so many years, she froze. Three times, she rang in with the wrong answer. She found the first Daily Double of the game, and then missed that, too. By the time the initial Jeopardy! round wrapped up and Trebek sent the show to commercials, Sausville was in the red with a score of negative $200, to her competitors' respective $3,600 and $2,000.

"I remember standing there during the commercial break, just feeling sorry for myself," Sausville says. "And thinking, *Oh, I wish I could just leave right now. Everybody's going to see this and they're going to see how I failed.*"

For Sausville, the stakes during her game felt especially high: Her husband, Justin Sausville, had appeared on *Jeopardy!* four years earlier and won six games and $134,000. "I think I felt especially negative about it because I knew that a lot of people on the show would perceive me as Justin's wife," she says, "and I didn't want to make women, wives, et cetera, look bad or undeserving of being there."

In the end, she shook off her early struggles. She ran a category to open Double Jeopardy!, bet big in Final Jeopardy!, and went on to win five games—making the Sausvilles the winningest married couple in *Jeopardy!* history, having both made it to the Tournament of Champions.

In the years since her appearance, Sausville has become something of a mentor to fellow *Jeopardy!* alumni—particularly women. In 2015, she co-founded a Facebook group for female *Jeopardy!* contestants with fellow champion Jennifer Morrow.

As is regrettably often the case for women who appear in a public forum, female *Jeopardy!* contestants are sometimes subjected to a startling amount of nastiness after their episodes go on the air. Some are inundated with threatening or lewd messages from strangers—the women's group keeps a list of "known creepers" that it warns new members to be wary of—or endure discussions of their appearance on social media.

During *Jeopardy!*'s orientation, contestant coordinators caution new players not to search for their names after their episodes air, but even those who refrain sometimes experience viewers tracking them down to share their decidedly unwelcome thoughts.

A year after her run, Morrow described in a podcast with Andy Saunders of *The Jeopardy! Fan* her shock at the amount of vitriol she encountered after she won two games in 2015.

Morrow brought an energetic, personality-forward approach to her games. Realizing that this was not exactly the norm on *Jeopardy!*, she expected some pushback. "I have thick skin, I can take it," she told Saunders.

But the reality was far worse than she imagined. Among other things, viewers tracked her down on social media just to tell her that they hated her. "I can't imagine hating a television contestant that much, with that much intensity," she said. "But people do, and that was something I really hadn't expected—being at the center of such a viciousness."

The problem has grown starker in recent years. Social media has made it ever easier both to express a harsh opinion and to reach the subject of it, a phenomenon experienced by everyone from Arthur Chu, who was the target of widespread abuse online after his 2014 run, to Viraj Mehta.

Mehta was an undergraduate at Stanford when he competed in the 2017 College Championship, during which he inadvertently seemed to flip off the camera while explaining to Trebek the differential geometry behind folding a piece of pizza. (He didn't mean to do it, he assures me.) The moment swiftly went viral, and then just as swiftly morphed from enjoyment of a moment Mehta himself calls "hilarious" to personal attacks, many of them racist.

As the story of his alleged bird-flipping was aggregated far and wide, from *E! News* to the *Daily Mail* to the *New York Daily News*, Mehta says that just a single reporter reached out to ask him what had actually happened.

Other players have also found themselves unable to correct the record when a *Jeopardy!* moment took off online. In the fall of 2019, Andrew Thomson won two games. In his third, a $200 clue appeared: "In *A Beautiful Day in the Neighborhood*, beloved children's TV show host Mister Rogers is played by this beloved actor," it read, alongside a clip of the little-known thespian Tom Hanks.

Alas, there was a buzzer malfunction at this point in the taping that prevented Thomson and his fellow contestants from ringing in. For home audiences, however, it appeared that this moment had been a triple stumper: Somehow, none of the three could recognize perhaps the most beloved actor of his generation. The moment exploded—as Thomson, who attempted in vain to explain what had happened on Twitter the night the episode aired, puts it, "social media, news sites, morning shows, and late-night TV thought we were history's greatest monsters and the most pop-culturally-inept trio of all time."

Hanks himself responded to it during an appearance on *Jimmy Kimmel Live!*: "You are kidding me!" he exclaimed. "You are kidding me! They didn't even have any wrong [guesses]?"

Even Jennings, now a decisive fan favorite, attracted plenty of derision during his initial run. My own boss at *The Ringer*, Bill Simmons, penned a column in *ESPN The Magazine* midway through Jennings's winning streak in which he proclaimed him "a smarmy know-it-all with the personality of a hall monitor, the kind of guy everyone hides from at a Christmas party." (Jennings didn't take it too hard—he uses the quote on the bio page of his website, where he suggested it was a continuation of "America's long national struggle between jocks and nerds." Sixteen years later, his company is still called Hall Monitor, LLC.)

For many contestants, the experience of going on *Jeopardy!* and of the backlash that sometimes follows is both surreal and isolating. Now, when new contestants appear on the show, Sausville, Morrow, and others often reach out directly, inviting them to groups for *Jeopardy!* alumni, sometimes even before their episodes have aired.

"We really try to make as many people as possible feel like there's more than just being on the show—there's this whole *Jeopardy!* alumni community that's there for you, and that understands what you've been through," Morrow told Saunders. "All the weirdness of it, of being on TV and having strangers hate you, all of the feelings of trying to process what just happened."

As Morrow put it, "Now we all have backup, which is a good feeling."

Unlike a lot of *Jeopardy!* champions, Pam Mueller didn't come up through competitive trivia circles. She was a junior at Loyola University Chicago when she decided to try out for the 2000 College Tournament, which she won, she says, to her enduring surprise. She came back for two more tournaments shortly afterward, the 2001 Tournament of Champions and the 2005 Ultimate Tournament of Champions.

"After the Ultimate Tournament of Champions, I got invited to O'Brien's Pub when I was out in LA," she says, and one thing led to another. She relocated to Los Angeles for work and can now be found at O'Brien's just about every week; she and Rutter, who won the Ultimate Tournament of Champions, have become close friends.

It turned out that *Jeopardy!* didn't exist in a vacuum at all. For Mueller, the very existence of the trivia world, with its competitive circuit, oddball jargon, and geeky gatherings, was a revelation. "It was this subcommunity that I didn't really know existed," she says.

"Even after I won the college tournament," continues Mueller, "I figured I'd do the Tournament of Champions and then that would be over. It would be a really cool story for the rest of my life."

So certain was she that *Jeopardy!* was a one-off (okay, two-off) that when the show auctioned off pieces of the set in 2002, she bought one of the contestant podiums for about $3,000 to have a permanent keepsake—only to find herself being invited to play on the new set again and again, including at the Battle of the Decades in 2014 and at 2019's All-Star Games.

"I wasn't particularly determined to get 'my' podium, but at that point in my *Jeopardy!* tenure, I had never been at podium no. 1, so I preferred 2 or 3," she says. "I figured I'd start bidding on 3, and if I lost, I'd try for 2. Brad [Rutter] had also placed an early bid on podium no. 1, and bidding against a millionaire seemed ill-advised."

At Trivia Nationals, Mueller is a bona fide celebrity. We sat down to chat in the back row of a ballroom, and within minutes a steady stream of fans arrived, many shyly approaching to ask if they could please take a picture with her, or shake her hand, or even just say hello. She first attended Trivia Nationals back in 2014, when the conference was under a different name, the Trivia Championships of North America, and has been a regular ever since.

What is it, I ask her, that keeps so many *Jeopardy!* alumni—even those who don't get offered chances to come back and play again—revolving in the show's orbit years after their appearances?

It isn't just the shared experience of having been on the show, or the shock of money or fame that it brought. If that were all, surely *Jeopardy!* wouldn't be the only game show to inspire this level of devotion from alumni.

Jeopardy!, Mueller says, is "the smart-person game show." Even in the heyday of *Who Wants to Be a Millionaire*, when that show became a *Jeopardy!*-esque proving ground for the trivially inclined, *Jeopardy!* was the better test: It had harder questions, and more of them. Mueller went on *Millionaire* in 2012 and won $25,000, but it wasn't the same. "I don't even know who was taping that day," she says.

In a strange way, it might be about the *lack* of competition. *Jeopardy!* is competitive, of course; if winning didn't matter, then the people in second and third place would keep their winnings, too. You go on *Jeopardy!* to win.

But by the time you go on *Jeopardy!*—well, you've gotten on *Jeopardy!* You've passed the first contestant test, then the one at the audition, and then convinced the contestant coordinators that you had something they thought millions of people would want to see.

Maybe you built a buzzer simulator or filled out thousands of flash cards, maybe you chugged a cup of coffee in the green room to help your reflexes, maybe you just showed up in Culver City after a lifetime of being the kid who knew things. However you did it, you did, and how could all the others who also, somehow, did the same exact thing not get it? How could all the people still trying to do it, honing their thumb timing on ballpoint pens and rehearsing the most dramatic versions of how they got engaged, studying opera or mythology or (ugh) sports every day when they get home from work, not see it, get it, and want in, too?

David Madden, the nineteen-time champion, remembers auditioning in the *Jeopardy!* studio in May 2004. With him was a friend named Jeff Hoppes, who was called to be on the show just before Madden and ultimately became one of the final victims of Ken Jennings, coming in second in the seventieth game of Jennings's seventy-four-game winning streak. Hoppes, Madden says, first played quiz bowl in high school when he was a classmate of Rutter's, and then went on to marry eventual six-time *Jeopardy!* champion and Tournament of Champions runner-up Larissa Kelly. Madden, Rutter, and Kelly made up the winning team in the All-Star Games.

"This whole world is kind of smaller than you think," Madden says. "You'd think with a country of 330 million people there wouldn't be quite as many connections, and yet.

"It is a very small *Jeopardy!* world," he concludes.

CHAPTER EIGHT

WHAT'S NEXT?

As a rule, a television soundstage is a cacophonous place, and so it is with *Jeopardy!*

On tape days, the wings are full of hurry: cameras wheeling *thump-thump-thump*, stagehands trying to figure out where so-and-so disappeared to, everyone talking into headsets and blaring alerts from the control booth to the stage to the dressing room, fiddling with the packs hooked to their belts and saying can you *believe* that bulb just blew out, coordinators telling a dozen lockjawed brainiacs to stand just exactly there and look at *this* camera, and—*hey!*—watch out for that cable.

But then you're led to a little door backstage and it opens, and inside is a tiny, peaceful nook of a room. The cold, electric air of the stage is replaced by a warm, golden glow. The walls are a sponge-painted pastel—art, honest-to-God art, hangs from the walls, and all the shouts and beeps and bangs from outside are suddenly muffled down to almost nothing. It's barely big enough for a desk and a chair, but you wonder if maybe you could live here, or at the very least take a nap. It is the office of Harry Friedman.

At *Jeopardy!*, the executive producer is the boss. Friedman has been doing it for a very long time: He became the producer of *Wheel of Fortune* in 1995, then added *Jeopardy!* two years later before becoming EP of both shows in 1999.

With supervising producers running much of the day-to-day action, particularly on *Jeopardy!* where episodes rarely diverge from their normal format, Friedman has been responsible for the bigger changes. He's the one who came up with the Clue Crew, who doubled the clue values during the *Who Wants to Be a Millionaire* mania, who made *Wheel* and *Jeopardy!* the first syndicated shows to broadcast in high definition, who pushed to start streaming episodes on platforms like Netflix and Hulu.

During taping, he sits at the judges' table, always in his same black leather jacket, partly to watch the episodes come together and partly to see if something, somewhere isn't quite right, is skipped or crooked or just generally un-*Jeopardy!*, and then stand up and tell everyone to stop and fix it.

"He's responsible for making the show exactly what it is today," says Cory Anotado, the founder of the game-show serial *BuzzerBlog*. "Without him at the helm of *Jeopardy!*, I don't think it would have lasted as long as it did through the '90s and the 2000s."

I should say, perhaps, that Friedman *sat* at the judges' table, that it *was* his warm, golden office. As Season 36 began, Friedman announced that it would be his last: Once taping wrapped in the spring of 2020, he would bid farewell to *Jeopardy!* and

Wheel. Not a retirement, he was quick to say, but, at seventy-three, at the very least a chance to step back, slow down. Months after his announcement, he would be honored with his own star on the Hollywood Walk of Fame.

When we sat down together in the midst of the All-Star Games, he was beaming, his latest madcap idea finally coming together: All the show's favorite players, the best and the most popular, right there in one place. That the show even knows that there are favorites is something new: the result of social media. There, players like Leonard Cooper and Austin Rogers, who in a practice round accidentally shouted "Fuck!" after missing a clue and then, realizing the error, covered his mouth and exclaimed, "Shit!," have developed vocal fan bases.

"It's been such a boon to us as producers because we get instant feedback—we don't have to engage in all kinds of complicated audience research," Friedman says. "But whilst not scientific, it's also very real and very, very, very useful and unfiltered."

It was Friedman's idea to take those discoveries—the idea that individual players, not just the show, had fans—and combine them with a fantasy-sports-inspired bracket that let viewers, and not a few show staff members, build their own pre-taping rosters. If *Jeopardy!* die-hards were sifting through advanced statistics hidden in all these episodes, why not lean in?

Friedman's exit from the show would be a seismic event at any time. That it coincides with the retirement of Maggie Speak, the show's beloved contestant coordinator, makes it all the more so. "She's like everyone's mom," one *Jeopardy!* staffer told me of Speak.

Friedman, for his part, made light of what his departure

might mean for the show. "I'm sure there will be changes," he said, then added with a smile: "Whatever changes there will be, will be after I'm in the South of France."

His exit came, too, as host Alex Trebek found himself in a battle with advanced pancreatic cancer, following his diagnosis in March 2019. While Trebek continued to host the show throughout his treatment, he was approaching his eightieth birthday as Season 36 wound down. Longtime announcer Johnny Gilbert, meanwhile, was nearly ninety-two.

Trebek and Gilbert proved unflappable, anchoring the show from the revival's very first episode, and as the years and episodes went by, the pair continued to wave off any hint of impending retirement. "It ticks me off," the host lamented of his spectacles-free partner. "I've needed glasses for half my life now."

But at some point, someday, they would step back. Season 37 would have a new executive producer for the first time in a quarter century, and a new head of its contestant department. Change, in short, is coming to *Jeopardy!*

For *Jeopardy!*, there was a real sense of worry in considering a future without Trebek as host—one heightened by the staff's affection for a man many had come to regard as a member of their extended family. After the show's second season wrapped, Harry Eisenberg remembered dousing the host—then also the producer—with a bucket of used Post-its, "since we didn't have any Gatorade."

"It's so hard to know," Friedman told me of what *Jeopardy!* would look like after Trebeck, "because we've never known any other host, so it's really hard to compare. We think the show will go on, but will it be the same? Will it be different? Probably."

The show will go on, of course. It remains a ratings
sensation: Through the first ten weeks of 2020, it led or tied
for the lead of all syndicated shows; when the Greatest of All
Time tournament aired in prime time on ABC in early 2020,
the episodes topped the viewership for nearly all television
programming in the previous year, including the first four
games of the 2019 NBA Finals and the first five games of the
2019 World Series. *Jeopardy!* is a juggernaut.

Trebek long insisted that it was the game that kept viewers
coming back, not him. "My success to a great extent has depended on the success of the game," he said midway through
the GOAT tournament's run. "You could've put somebody
else in as the host of *Jeopardy!* thirty-six years ago—not everybody, but there are some individuals who could have been
named as host of *Jeopardy!*, and if the show had lasted thirty-
six years, they would be enjoying the same kind of favorable
reviews and adulation that I have enjoyed in recent years."

Not everybody, indeed.

⟵

If the question is *How do you replace the irreplaceable?*,
the answer is obvious: You can't. Trebek was a singular
presence—on *Jeopardy!*, on television, and in homes across
North America.

His death in November 2020, from complications of pancreatic cancer, prompted an intense outpouring of grief among his
legions of fans, as well as those who had worked with him.

"It's just so hard to imagine it without Alex," Jon Cannon,
who was a member of the *Jeopardy!* Clue Crew from 2005
to 2009, told me weeks after Trebek's death. "The show has

been reliably good for a generation. So to imagine it as being anything other than what it's been is difficult to do."

The loss loomed especially large for the people who suddenly found themselves on a set without him. For Zach Newkirk, who returned to *Jeopardy!* a month after Trebek's death to defend a winning streak originally interrupted when the COVID-19 pandemic shut down production that spring, the freshness of Trebek's absence was palpable onstage, where Newkirk's taping was, he says, just "the third day after Alex." During one of the show's midgame Q&As between Ken Jennings, then serving as the show's inaugural guest host, and contestants, Newkirk accidentally invoked Trebek. "He said, 'So you're a voting rights attorney?' and I said, 'That's right, Alex,'" Newkirk says. The mixup was edited out and retaped.

"I felt really bad and embarrassed, but [Jennings] was such a great sport about it," Newkirk says. "He said, 'If there's anyone I could hope to be compared to, it would be Alex Trebek, so it's really an honor.'" In the version that aired, Newkirk said, "That's right, Ken." When a crew member also slipped up later in the day and called Jennings "Alex" without seeming to notice the mistake, Newkirk says Jennings turned to him and raised his eyebrows, as if to say, *See?*

Trebek was long clear on one count: He would not be involved in choosing his eventual successor. "It's not a decision that would be up to me, and I would not make myself available to presenting an opinion," he told me. "I would leave it up to the people in charge."

This, perhaps, had something to do with his own experience taking over *Jeopardy!* In 1987, original host Art Fleming griped that Trebek's edition had easier material and was unfair to its contestants. "There are too many lights," Fleming complained of the new show. "It's too slick." Trebek, it seems, wanted the next host to be able to make the show their own.

"Obviously," Trebek told me, "they're going to look at somebody younger, somebody personable, someone who appears to be intelligent, who appears to be friendly and kindly disposed toward the contestants."

Through it all, the question that loomed at Sony was how much of *Jeopardy!*'s success depended on Trebek's presence. On the one hand, Fleming's version, too, was a hit. But the show's attempts at spin-offs—*Rock & Roll Jeopardy!* and the children's version *Jep!* in 1998, *Sports Jeopardy!* in 2014— were all short-lived. Each had much of the *Jeopardy!* production team, including Friedman as executive producer, behind them, and relative star power in their hosts: Probst on *Rock & Roll* just before he took on the pilot of the mega-successful *Survivor*, former *SportsCenter* anchor Dan Patrick on *Sports Jeopardy!* (plus then–Clue Crew member Kelly Miyahara as the announcer), and the voice of Porky Pig, Bob Bergen, on *Jep!*

Their failures can be attributed to a lot of things, including their hyper-specificity and perhaps their platforms (*Sports Jeopardy!* debuted on the little-known streaming platform Crackle). But they might also point, worryingly, to the idea that the *Jeopardy!* formula alone is not enough to make a show succeed—that it needs whatever magic Trebek and Fleming before him were able to provide. There was precedent, after all, for the bottom suddenly falling out for even the most popular of game shows. *Who Wants to Be a Millionaire* was a smash hit under Regis Philbin, but less than two years later its ratings were in a downward spiral from which the show would never recover.

It was a conundrum that could scarcely have mattered more to parent studio Sony. *Jeopardy!* and *Wheel of Fortune* are consistently among the top-rated syndicated shows on TV, and together they bring in a reported $125 million in profit each year. Sony's television business produces "substantially higher" profits than its movie arm, according to Ben Fritz's 2018 Sony deep dive, *The Big Picture. Wheel* and *Jeopardy!*, Fritz wrote, "have made total profits of $2 billion and $1 billion, respectively, over their decades on the air."

Meredith Vieira holds the record for longest-serving female game show host, thanks to her eleven years with *Millionaire*; she has since hosted *25 Words or Less*, an adaptation of the board game. The version of *Millionaire* that she took over was different from the outset—a daytime syndicated edition cut from an hour to a punchier half-hour slice—but it was still a show that in its early years was closely associated with Philbin.

"People would say to me at the time, 'Those are big shoes to fill,' and my attitude was, Well, I'm not trying to fill his shoes," Vieira said in a conversation in early 2020. "I'm trying to feel comfortable in my own. Nobody else is going to be Regis, but by the same token, nobody else is going to be me, so I had to just bring to that show whatever my particular strengths were."

Vieira conceded that Trebek was bound to be "certainly a tough act to follow, because of everything he has brought to the game. But I think he'd be the first one to say this should go on.

"I think he sees this is a show, as they say, with legs," she said. "I don't think any host is bigger than the show, and any good host doesn't want to be. It's about the game."

At the All-Star Games, Jennings was quick to admit that whatever came next would be hard for *Jeopardy!* "For thirty-five years nobody's ever seen anyone else do it. It's going to be like the Bob Barker situation. I think it's tricky for the show."

Nearly a year before he would find himself behind the lectern, he also made a hosting promise. "If I were called upon to fill it, I would obviously have to serve my country and my game show," he said.

———

If you thought James Holzhauer could finally be talked into donning a sport coat to hold court with broadcast big-wigs—well.

It's January in Southern California, and the three most successful players in *Jeopardy!* history—Holzhauer, Jennings, and Rutter—are lounging in a leafy Pasadena courtyard.

They've just finished their Q&A panel with that ballroom of TV critics, all in search of quotes about the Greatest of All Time tournament. More than a few of those in the audience, it seems, were devoted *Jeopardy!* fans, at times shouting over one another as the three contestants, Friedman, and Trebek squinted into the lights to see who had asked about buzzer strategy, or the show's legacy, or—oh my goodness—if Trebek ever swears off-camera. Rutter says that one reporter approached him later and professed it the greatest panel he'd ever seen.

Holzhauer—who, true to form, wears a maroon sweater while his fellow contestants sport blazers and ties—looks a little shell-shocked by the attention. "James is in the middle of the whirlwind of it and I keep telling him it's going to be okay," Jennings says jovially.

Jennings, who had joked that any proceeds from the tournament would go toward purchasing Holzhauer a coat "and maybe even a necktie," kept his word, shipping the runner-up both shortly after the contest's finale aired. "You may not have seen either of these things before, but you should be able to find videos online," he wrote in a note. "Wishing you all the great things you deserve in your post-*Jeopardy!* life!" When the tournament re-aired in the spring with video commentary from the contestants at home, Holzhauer—content as always to play the peevish little brother with his quiz-show elders— donned both over (what else?) a V-neck undershirt, the tie fastened haphazardly around his throat.

For Jennings, the fame has become more manageable as the memory of his seventy-four-game winning streak has gradually receded. Now, he says, the interactions are less frequent, if not exactly rare: "It becomes one person a day whistling the theme at you in the mall," he jokes.

Sometimes, he says, someone on the street will stop him and immediately throw out a trivia question, apparently memorized on the off chance they might someday bump into a worthy target: "I don't know why they would do that," he adds. But life has mostly returned to normal, or at least a post-*Jeopardy!* kind of normal. Days pass with nary a mention of signaling devices.

Holzhauer, on the other hand, was then in the midst of his third *Jeopardy!* appearance in the nine months since the beginning of his own streak, and any sort of return to anonymity is hard to imagine happening anytime soon. Earlier that week, all three players were in New York City to tape a segment on the tournament with *Good Morning America*. Twice, they were passed by a stranger; twice, that stranger pointed only at Holzhauer, said "*Jeopardy!* guy!," and carried on.

"Brad and I were like, '*Hey*,'" Jennings says in mock-offense.

"Well, you were," says Rutter, wryly. "I'm used to it." Rutter, whose well-cut suits and carefully cropped beard give him the look of someone who might be dubbed "*Jeopardy!*'s super-stylish mega-champion" by *Vanity Fair*—which he was—is decidedly the least recognizable of the three. His initial run came before the five-game limit was lifted, meaning that although he is by far the show's most decorated player—he is the all-time winnings leader with five tournament victories and nearly $5 million to his name—he never saw the media frenzy that Holzhauer and Jennings did.

Life has changed for all three since their *Jeopardy!* reigns first began. Jennings, who had been muddling through work as a computer programmer in Salt Lake City, Utah, quit his job, became an author, and moved with his family to Seattle, Washington. (He was born in nearby Edmonds.)

Rutter was twenty-two and working at a record store in his hometown of Lancaster, Pennsylvania, when he taped his first episode in 2000. He also left his job, and eventually decamped for Los Angeles and an acting career. (He jokes that he might not have had that much of a choice on the change-of-profession front, given that the record store has since closed: "I would have been laid off, so I don't know, I probably would've learned to code.")

For now, Holzhauer is still doing more or less what he was before *Jeopardy!* and placing sports bets at the Westgate in Las Vegas, but he hints that that is likely to change soon enough.

"I think it'd be interesting to be in this game-show space," he says, coyly, though he laments that he may never get invited on *Sesame Street*, as Jennings was after his run. Holzhauer grins, and makes a nod to some of the less charitable *Jeopardy!* viewers on social media: "I'm never going to get on *Sesame Street* with *my* mouth."

Just about everyone seems stiff on *Jeopardy!*, which by design lends about as little time as possible to character development. This is a show where self-expression on the part of contestants is limited to a sentence or two during the Q&A, maybe a grimace or self-conscious celebration if they land a Daily Double.

So it's hard to know what to make of players when they stick around. Are they smug? They sure *seem* smug, showing off all those perfectly useless facts, and getting rich to boot. A contestant on any given night of *Jeopardy!* feels at once familiar and totally foreign. *A five-day champion? In my* Jeopardy!*?* As Trebek said, it takes a little while to get to like somebody.

In the years since they first played, Jennings and Rutter have become unofficial spokespeople for *Jeopardy!*, perennially called upon by reporters to explain the latest viral clue or fast-buzzing contestant. They've also become pseudo-coaches, lending their advice or maybe just an ear to contestants training for their tape day, or those hoping to get the call in the first place, or those trying to make sense of a taping gone wrong.

In the months that I've been talking to *Jeopardy!* hopefuls, it's often only a matter of time before I hear: *So then I emailed Ken.* One *Jeopardy!* fan told me he once asked Rutter to lunch and, after Rutter—"dressed to the nines," of course— took him up on it, he insisted on paying for the game-show legend's meal.

"Even though they only pay us occasionally, we kind of

work for them," Rutter says of *Jeopardy!* "If we can be as welcoming as possible to people, then I think the show gets that reputation, too."

Rutter jokes that Holzhauer—who likes to say his dream is to be a pro wrestling heel, a spirit embraced on his oft-salty Twitter feed—is unlikely to find himself in a similar guidance role. " 'Hey James, how do I get good at *Jeopardy!*?' " he imagines a contestant in training writing him. " 'I don't know, be as good as me?' "

While the GOAT tournament was positioned as something of a swan song for the three players, it's unlikely to be the last audiences see of them, for the simple reason that for many viewers, they're synonymous with *Jeopardy!* And audiences' interest in *Jeopardy!* shows little sign of abating.

"Millions of Americans love trivia, and this is the peak of it," Jennings says. "This is the place where it intersects with pop culture and respectability."

Holzhauer nods. "If you watch an NBA game on TV, you don't think, *Oh, I can dunk over LeBron*," he says. "But you might think, *Oh, I could get a question here or there if the right categories come up*."

Rutter calls it "the original interactive TV," and it is. As much as *Jeopardy!* is a game among three people, it is at least as much about the unseen thousands—millions—playing their own games in their own spaces, competing against the people onstage, the people next to them, or perhaps just against themselves.

Like so many contestants before and after him, back in 2000, Rutter simply wanted to say he had been there. "That was my goal going on the show," he says. "I just wanted to win one game so I could say I was a *Jeopardy!* champion."

AFTERWORD TO THE
TRADE EDITION

On an overcast morning in August 2021, a group of studio executives, television producers, and some of the most important champions in *Jeopardy!* history gathered with the family of Alex Trebek on the Sony Pictures lot in Culver City.

It was the first tape day of the quiz show's thirty-eighth season—and the first time in nearly four decades without the legendary host at the helm.

Trebek's death the previous year after a brutal fight with pancreatic cancer had devastated his fans, family, and the longtime staff of a show he had built into an American institution. That morning, those assembled planned to rechristen the *Jeopardy!* set as the Alex Trebek Stage.

For executives at the show and its parent studio, Sony, Trebek's passing also threatened what had been for decades one of the few sure bets in television: a cultural touchstone with an exceedingly loyal fan base, low production costs, and consistently spectacular ratings.

But—improbably—as the group assembled that morning for the ceremonial unveiling of the renamed stage, the venerable game show appeared, at least to the outside world, stronger than ever.

In the aftermath of Trebek's death, *Jeopardy!* executives settled on a novel approach to finding his replacement: a seven-month rolling audition that would see some of entertainment's biggest stars get their shot behind the host lectern.

The hope was that the rotating collection of stars would keep the show in the public conversation, while drawing in new viewers who could root for celebrities they already loved.

And largely, the effort worked. NFL fans tuned in to see Green Bay Packers quarterback Aaron Rodgers take his turn behind the lectern—a stint that prompted weeks of speculation on ESPN debate shows over whether a future Hall of Famer might walk away from football to host a game show. Millennials who grew up with *Reading Rainbow* and *Star Trek* star LeVar Burton rallied behind his candidacy online, flooding social media with memes begging for him to be selected as the next host. Regular viewers of NBC's *Today* show and ABC's *Good Morning America* were drawn into the competition, as current and former anchors Katie Couric, Savannah Guthrie, Robin Roberts, and George Stephanopoulos took them behind the scenes. *The Big Bang Theory* actress Mayim Bialik, who earned a doctorate in neuroscience, won a following with her quirky delivery, while journalists and broadcasters like Joe Buck, Anderson Cooper, David Faber, Sanjay Gupta, and Bill Whitaker brought prime-time polish. Even controversial choices, like discredited television doctor Mehmet Oz, generated conversation and coverage.

The competition in the games was as fierce as the one among those vying to replace Trebek. Matt Amodio, a Yale graduate student studying computer science, had kicked off one of the most impressive streaks in the show's history, concluding the previous season on an eighteen-day winning streak. With more than $500,000 already in hand, new records, including the potential to top the streaks of celebrated champions Julia Collins and James Holzhauer, were now in spitting distance. Between Amodio's historic run and the previous season's hosting competition, there was a focus on and interest in *Jeopardy!* far exceeding anything in the show's history.

Leading that Thursday's ceremony was the man who had emerged victorious from the search for a permanent host: executive producer Mike Richards.

Richards, who had taken over *Jeopardy!* and its sister show *Wheel of Fortune* as executive producer in 2020, was an unlikely choice. He had some experience in front of the camera, including a stint hosting *Beauty and the Geek*, but he wasn't well known to the general public—particularly compared to some of the A-list guest hosts who had graced the *Jeopardy!* stage. His selection had prompted inevitable comparisons to Dick Cheney, who famously landed on himself as the best candidate while leading George W. Bush's search for a vice presidential running mate. On the heels of a contest that had encouraged fans to rally around their preferred host, disappointment swirled among those who saw their favorite passed over.

But Richards positioned himself as a feel-good underdog. He had sought the previous season to link himself to Trebek. Ahead of the first episode to air after Trebek's death, Richards delivered a short message from the side of the empty *Jeopardy!* stage. "Over the weekend, we lost our beloved host, Alex Trebek," he began, seeming to blink back tears. "This is an enormous loss for our staff and crew, for his family and for his millions of fans. He loved this show and everything it stood for." Richards pledged to air Trebek's remaining episodes, because "that's what he wanted."

And when Richards began his own guest hosting stint early in the audition rotation, he started a tradition of quoting the late host at the end of each episode. "As Alex said, we're trying to build a kinder and gentler society," he said. "And if we all pitch in just a little bit, we're going to get there. See you next time."

He told reporters he had only gotten a chance behind the lectern because other guest hosts were concerned about the pandemic or otherwise obligated—and that he wanted to make sure the show continued uninterrupted. The effort earned gushing coverage from Hollywood trades, which helped to propel his candidacy.

It also didn't hurt that Richards enjoyed a close relationship with Sony Pictures Entertainment CEO Tony Vinciquerra and Sony television chairman Ravi Ahuja, a relationship he had nurtured over his time producing the show. And by naming Bialik a special host for a series of prime-time tournaments on ABC planned for the coming year, the studio tempered criticism that it had selected another white man.

The ceremony that Thursday wouldn't quite be a coronation, but it wasn't far off. Trebek's wife and children crowded together for a picture beside a new plaque outside the soundstage with the name of the late host. Champions Ken Jennings and Buzzy Cohen, both of whom had taken turns as guest hosts, were on hand, with the first contestants of the new season straining to catch glimpses of them before their games. Amodio settled in for the usual morning orientation, uncomfortably aware of the fact that, unlike during his earlier games, his new opponents now knew exactly who he was.

But there was a problem.

By the time the first games of the season would tape later

that day, long-brewing anger and distrust of Richards would erupt into the open as revelations about his past comments and behavior exploded into the public eye. A meeting between Richards and the show's senior staff grew heated. By its end, according to multiple sources close to *Jeopardy!*, several were uncertain that they would have a job to return to the next day.

On the most important day in the quiz show's recent history, *Jeopardy!* was in chaos.

The first time I interviewed Richards, he called me from his car.

For twenty minutes, we talked about the slew of COVID-19 safety measures that the show had introduced to restart production in the summer of 2020, from detached contestant lecterns to a recording studio that the *Jeopardy!* crew had rigged for then–ninety-two-year-old Johnny Gilbert in his home.

It was Trebek, Richards said as he made his way through the Los Angeles traffic, who had most enthusiastically nagged him to get the show back into production.

"His frustration was, we should be in there taping," Richards said. "We should be shooting. Even though it was during our hiatus, he wanted to get back in there and shoot more *Jeopardy!*'s. So I was definitely hearing him on my shoulder, going, 'Let's go. Figure it out. We're *Jeopardy!* We're smart enough to figure this out.'"

As the conversation wound down, I asked what I figured would be a softball: Would we see a Tournament of Champions at some point?

"We are very motivated to—uh—do a Tournament of Champions this year," he began, haltingly.

Then he stopped. "Um—and—sorry, give me one second—let me just—" he said, his voice strained.

I heard his turning signal flip on.

"Take your time," I said. He went silent. *Click-click. Click-click.* It went on this way for an amount of time I would categorize as "worrying."

Then his side went silent. *Oh my God*, I thought. *I'm going to get the executive producer of* Jeopardy! *bulldozed by oncoming traffic.*

Richards, however, emerged unscathed, and, indeed, the show successfully hosted a Tournament of Champions that spring. He thanked me before we hung up for being "a supporter of the show."

"I will keep bothering you in the future, I'm sure," I said.

"Perfect," he replied. "That would be great."

As it happened, I hadn't planned to still be writing about *Jeopardy!* at all at that point.

By November 2020, as the hardcover edition of this book was about to be published, I'd spent two years reporting on the show. I had gotten to know contestants and the *Jeopardy!* staff, and I'd meant the book as a tribute to the show's legions of hardcore fans.

But, joyful as the reporting process often was, after all those months in the NaCl mines, I was ready to be done with the quiz show. *I don't want to be the* Jeopardy! *person forever*, I told anyone who would listen.

Unlike so many of the people I interviewed, I hadn't grown up nursing dreams of one day getting a shot as a contestant, and I was far from a bar trivia regular. I *liked Jeopardy!*, and I now counted many of the show's obsessives among my friends. I'd even, begrudgingly, begun to say "lectern" instead of "podium." But I was ready to move on.

In the weeks leading up to the release of *Answers in the Form of Questions*, I was back to reporting an eclectic mix of stories for *The Ringer*—everything from how haunted houses were adapting during the pandemic to profiles of animal trainers on Hollywood sets.

Friends asked if I was considering another book—maybe the history of *Wheel of Fortune*, more than a few asked with a grin. No, I would answer. But I did start kicking the tires on other projects, at one point even buying a collection of memoirs by professional sports mascots to see if there was a story to tell about the indelible mark the Phillie Phanatic, Mr. Met, and Crazy Crab had left on American life.

All I needed to do was get through publication and a handful of promotional interviews, and then I would be done with *Jeopardy!*, perhaps for good.

And then, on November 8, two days before my book's release, my phone buzzed with the news that Trebek had died that morning.

I had interviewed Trebek while working on the book, and I had spent days on the *Jeopardy!* set observing him in his longtime habitat. But I didn't know him well. He was, famously, a cipher, especially to contestants, who were barred from behind-the-scenes contact with him in deference to FCC regulations about game show objectivity.

Still, I had come to know many of those who had spent years

working by his side. In the weeks after his death, I called sports-caster Dan Patrick, who had hosted *Sports Jeopardy!* in the 2010s and who told me about Trebek taking him out to dinner after he was hired and gifting him one of the grease pencils that the host favored to mark his answer key in the midst of a game. I talked to Ace Miller, a former police officer who long ran security for *Jeopardy!* and *Wheel of Fortune*, who grumbled fondly about Trebek's propensity to take questions from anyone and every-one and tell them whatever they wanted to know, even personal details that made a security detail's job that much harder.

I met Madison Moore and Brandt Sherman, two friends who'd stumbled across Trebek's phone number and then spent a decade intermittently prank-calling him. Moore and Sherman began a tradition of calling Trebek from friends' wedding ceremonies to ask for his blessing, which he invari-ably provided. "I hope you're half as lucky as I am," he told one groom. "I don't know who you are, I don't know where you are, but if you're getting married, I'll just wish you good luck," he told another. He never hung up first, they said.

I spoke to Kelly Miyahara, formerly of the Clue Crew, who told me about Trebek creeping into the background of a shot she was filming in the Galápagos Islands to lie facedown amidst a group of dozing sea lions, and the time the *Jeopardy!* staff used a down day in Italy to take a trip to Pompeii, where Trebek had spent the whole time peppering their tour guide with questions.

"It's hard to believe, I think, because I haven't been at the show," she said of Trebek's absence from the set. "I hadn't seen him in person in a really long time, and somewhere I still feel like he's there."

Like Miyahara, I too found myself struggling to think of the host in the past tense. Suddenly, my book had become something more than a deep dive into the show—it was a look into the legacy of the man who had hosted it for more than thirty-six years. My inbox, and then my calendar, filled.

COVID-19 was still ravaging the country, so I recorded cable news segments about Trebek's life and legacy from my living room. I got hissed at by a Canadian radio host when my doorbell exploded just as I was introduced live, and I begged—*begged*—producers to please not make me answer any more queries in the form of a question.

I hosted a digital panel of *Jeopardy!* greats—Cohen, Holzhauer, Pam Mueller, Austin Rogers, and Brad Rutter—at the 92Y in New York City, with, I later learned, my supremely lumpy cat grooming herself with maximum grotesqueness just behind me. We asked the venue to not allow audience questions about who should succeed Trebek.

But in the ensuing months, I, like the rest of the nation, became enthralled by the search for the next host.

As celebrity guest hosts rotated through Culver City in rolling auditions, I dug back into the *Jeopardy!* beat. I interviewed Rodgers, who kicked off a surreal wave of NFL free agent gossip when he told me that he thought he could both host *Jeopardy!* full time and keep playing in the NFL.

I learned that Guthrie apologized to a contestant off-camera for having to correct her pronunciation during a game— *Jeopardy!* demands that Trebekian edge, like it or not—and that it took Oz a half-dozen tries to pronounce "antidisestablish-mentarianism" as players rolled their eyes across the studio.

I taught a national radio host how to pronounce the name "Mayim Bialik," who said that the intensity of hosting *Jeopardy!* was "second only to giving birth to my second son on the floor of my living room."

I saw the fandom roiled by new factions: the *Jeopardy!* stans who would countenance no one but Jennings or Cohen; the scores of *Reading Rainbow*, *Star Trek*, and *Roots* obsessives who rallied to support Burton's vocal campaign for the job; the viewers who found themselves suddenly obsessed with Faber, who won the heart of many a die-hard with his tales of wooing friends to play in practice games with pizza and wine.

Mostly, I studied the tea leaves about how *Jeopardy!* and Sony were approaching the search.

Virtually all the public information came from Richards, who quickly became *Jeopardy!*'s de facto spokesperson and the public face of the host search.

He had arrived at *Jeopardy!* and *Wheel of Fortune* in 2020, succeeding longtime executive producer Harry Friedman, who had been the two shows' creative linchpin for nearly twenty-five years. Richards came with a long list of game show accolades, and the industry hands I spoke to were optimistic about what he might bring as a showrunner.

He gave the impression that he viewed his job as something of a stewardship. "The great thing about *Jeopardy!* is that it's not broken," he told me. "I wasn't brought in because the show needed to be fixed."

As the host search began in earnest, he presented the studio's process as one anchored in objectivity.

"We want to go at this with real analytics and real testing and not just go, 'Hey, how about this guy?' which is kind of how a lot of these decisions have been made historically," he said on a *Wall Street Journal* podcast.

Sony has "the most robust team of people I have ever seen looking at this and analyzing it in a very cerebral way," he told the AP.

"I'm online every day looking at [the fan reaction] and checking it out," he said in *USA Today*.

To *Broadcasting & Cable*, he touted the studio's commitment to "data and analytics, testing and focus groups": "We aren't looking for a three-year host, we're looking for a ten-year or a twenty-year host," he said.

Then I began to hear whispers that Richards was gunning for the job himself. "I mean, it's the greatest job in television, although I may be biased," he said that May. "I would definitely consider it if Sony made that decision and wanted me to do it. It would be amazing."

Richards was a dark-horse candidate, to put it mildly.

That January, he had stepped in to guest host two weeks of games. At the time, he framed his appearance onstage as a last-minute rescue after Jennings, who had guest hosted the first six weeks of games after Trebek's final episodes, had a sudden conflict.

"We have some amazing guest hosts coming that I can't wait for you to see, but with the COVID outbreak here in LA, folks were understandably a little reticent to shoot," Richards said in a short preamble at the beginning of his first episode. "Ken Jennings did a great job, but he's unavailable due to obligations with his show *The Chase*."

Richards had told *Broadcasting & Cable* that he was "never meant to be a part of that [the guest-hosting] process. I was just meant to manage—but COVID had other plans."

That spring, he talked to me at length about the stress of finding himself suddenly stepping in.

"*Jeopardy!* for the host is nonstop intensity," he said, recounting his hurried attempts to shake up his on-camera tics, like saying "Correct!" after each contestant response.

"You want to get from chasing the train to trying to lead the train."

On August 11, Sony announced that Richards would be the show's new daily host. In a press release, Ahuja, the Sony TV chairman, emphasized that Richards and Bialik "were both at the top of our research and analysis."

"We took this decision incredibly seriously," Ahuja continued. "A tremendous amount of work and deliberation has gone into it, perhaps more than has ever gone into the selection of hosts for a show—deservedly so because it's *Jeopardy!* and we are following the incomparable Alex Trebek. A senior group of Sony Pictures Television executives pored over footage from every episode, reviewed research from multiple panels and focus groups, and got valuable input from our key partners and *Jeopardy!* viewers."

But none of this, it turned out, was totally accurate. That mascot research would have to wait.

On August 18, *The Ringer* published my investigation into the circumstances of Richards's hiring as host.

In reporting the piece, I spoke with people around *Jeopardy!* and Sony, as well as staff at the shows that Richards had executive produced before moving to Sony, *The Price Is Right* and *Let's Make a Deal.*

What emerged was a showrunner who could be vindictive and self-dealing—and one who was much more involved in the host decision than he or Sony had said publicly.

Sources told me that he was not actually an emergency fill-in for Jennings, who had been widely seen as the frontrunner for the job. They revealed the fact that Trebek, who had also asked Jennings to narrate much of the audiobook of his 2020 memoir, *The Answer Is . . .*, left him a pair of cuff links. They awaited Jennings in Trebek's dressing room with a note from Trebek's wife, Jean, when he arrived at the studio to guest host his first episode.

Instead, Richards pushed Jennings to the side, seizing a minor time conflict on an upcoming tape day that the show's production team had said they could accommodate to insist on hosting himself. Jennings, who had officially joined *Jeopardy!* as a consulting producer at the start of the 2020–2021 season, had spent the season's early months delivering occasional categories that he had written. After Richards stepped in to host, no Jennings category appeared again.

As executive producer, Richards had vast influence over the candidacies of all the other contenders, coaching them during their appearances and choosing which—if any—episodes to send on to the much-ballyhooed focus groups. In the case of Burton, Richards had opted to give him just a week behind the lectern, half the time that most other hosts received; that week fell in the midst of the Summer Olympics, pushing down those episodes' ratings. Richards's episodes, on the other hand, fell during a February "sweeps" period, a crucial and much-scrutinized window that influences advertiser purchasing. Far from being neutral and data-driven, the host search had been broken from the start, with a man who wanted the job for himself able to manipulate nearly every element of the competition.

I'd also found a podcast hosted by Richards several years earlier.

Curious about his early experiences on camera, I looked into a comedy show that he had created and emceed as a student at Pepperdine University in the 1990s. He mentioned it often in interviews, going so far as to feature it in his biography on *Jeopardy!*'s website: *The Randumb Show.*

"We named it *The Randumb Show*—D-U-M-B—because every person on campus at that time—the phrase was 'That is so *random*. Ugh, that's *random*,'" he told Pepperdine's president in an interview two months before he was tapped to host *Jeopardy!* "And so we were making fun of that."

His collegiate experiences in front of an audience were a professional turning point, he continued. "I learned you've got to create your own breaks," he said of college efforts at standup comedy. "I had to kind of force my way onto the stage. And that is the way you make it in television, too—you kind of force your way in."

Sufficiently intrigued, I began to look for episodes of the show. Instead, I found something quite a bit more recent: a podcast by the same name, which he had hosted in 2013 and 2014 while serving as the EP at *The Price Is Right.*

Bawdy and crude, Richards does not exactly come across as the thoughtful trivia guardian he'd taken pains to present himself as in interviews about *Jeopardy!* I began by choosing episodes at random, abbreviating the more than thirty hours of conversation by listening to them at 1.5 speed.

Midway through my listen, and in the midst of an oppressively humid Washington, DC, summer, my home's air conditioning unit suddenly died. With an ice pack on my stomach, I settled sweatily into my couch, idly wondering if Sony had sent appliance-sabotaging henchmen to throw me off course.

I kept listening. *Did he really say that?* I would ask myself, pausing to rewind at normal speed.

He did. Episodes featured discussions of women's bodies and sexist, racist, and ableist comments. In one episode, he asked his cohost—a much younger actress named Beth Triffon, who had previously worked as his assistant—if she had ever taken nude photos and asked to look through her phone. When she declined to share an image with him, he asked whether it was "of [her] boobies." He said that one-piece swimsuits were "genuinely unattractive" and had made the cohost's friends "look really frumpy and overweight." When a guest made a comment about big noses, Richards replied, "Ixnay on the ose-nay. She's not an ew-Jay."

His comments about women were particularly concerning. After emerging as the likely choice for host, new scrutiny was given to multiple lawsuits filed during Richards's time at *The Price Is Right*, which focused on the mistreatment of female employees by *Price*'s male leadership, including Richards. In one suit, Brandi Cochran, a former *Price* model, described Richards dictating what women on the show were told to wear. "Richards decided that the models' skirts should be shorter and said that he liked the models to look as if they were going out on a date," the suit read. "At his suggestion, models wore bikinis on the show more frequently."

It was hard not to find unfavorable comparisons to Trebek. Trebek, for one, was a vocal philanthropist and a long-time supporter of the Hope of the Valley Rescue Mission, a shelter in Northridge, California, to which he gave $500,000 shortly before his death. (*Jeopardy!* contributed an additional $250,000.)

Richards, however, seemed to take a different view. After finding out that his cohost had qualified for unemployment insurance benefits, he referred to the benefits as "crack" and asked, "Do you feel dirty? Seriously, and I'm not trying to be mean. Do you feel a little dirty?" When the cohost later said that she had given a dollar to an unhoused woman, Richards replied, "That's the sound of America going down the toilet."

Surreally, one episode of *The Randumb Show* even featured an interview with Jennings, to whom Richards declared his own unfitness for *Jeopardy!*

"If I had gotten on *Jeopardy!*—well, I never would have gotten on *Jeopardy!*, let's be square," he told Jennings.

Together with a team of *Ringer* editors, producers, and fact checkers, I began to put together what I had learned into a story: "A Smile with Sharp Teeth": Mike Richards's Rise to *Jeopardy!* Host Sparks Questions About His Past—a title derived from a description of Richards by a former *Let's Make a Deal* staffer who had worked under him. I reached out to Richards's agent and to Sony for comment ahead of publication, asking in part about *The Randumb Show*. In response, a Sony spokesperson said that the studio had been unaware of the podcast before I had asked about it. Within hours, every episode of the podcast was wiped from its online hosting site. (This, though, was surmountable: *The Ringer*'s audio team had pulled their own backup copies just in case.)

"It is humbling to confront a terribly embarrassing moment of misjudgment, thoughtlessness, and insensitivity from nearly a decade ago," Richards said in a statement. "Looking back now, there is no excuse, of course, for the comments I made on this podcast and I am deeply sorry."

The morning after my *Ringer* article published, the *Jeopardy!* staff convened at the set for the Alex Trebek Stage dedication.

Unease had been growing among the staff for months. The combination of Trebek's death, Friedman's exit, and the departures of several other key staff members—including the longtime head of the contestant department, Maggie Speak, and stage manager John Lauderdale—meant that Richards had arrived in a power vacuum.

Friedman's long tenure had allowed him to run *Jeopardy!* and *Wheel* as autonomous fiefdoms. Now Sony leadership— many of whose members were themselves relatively new to the studio—seemed to be responsible for decisions both big and small. As the year went on, the *Jeopardy!* staff learned of major news—including that Richards had been named host— along with the public in press releases and on social media.

By the morning of the dedication, the distrust between Richards and the show's staff had reached a crisis point. Each taping morning at *Jeopardy!* begins with a meeting between the executive producer, the host, supervising producers Lisa Broffman and Rocky Schmidt, a lawyer from an external compliance firm, and a group of writers and researchers including head writers Michele Loud and Billy Wisse.

These meetings, which are held in the encyclopedia-ringed writers' library, tend toward the prosaic: The group maps out the five games that will be played that day, occasionally debating clue wording or Daily Double placement. And then, in the words of Trebek, they go to work.

But this day was different.

Some of those present had seen the subterfuge with Jennings's hosting conflict play out in real time months earlier, and had watched with mounting concern as Richards lied on camera about the origins of his hosting turn. Others had been keenly aware of Richards's potentially problematic involvement in the guest-host auditions. And now they had been confronted with the clips from Richards's podcast.

Headlines about *Jeopardy!* being in crisis were everywhere; by the day's end, the Anti-Defamation League would call for an investigation and Stephen Colbert would rip into Richards on *The Late Show*, joking that his job might, yes, be in jeopardy.

Above all, according to multiple sources with knowledge of the meeting, staff members voiced concern that *Jeopardy!* had been irreparably tainted.

On American television, there is no other show quite like it. *Jeopardy!*, whose enormous audience and cultural currency is derived through some alchemy of its brainy format and its longevity and built-in nostalgia, is perhaps especially dependent on its unimpeachability in the public eye.

It was this point that had led much of the staff to feel an overwhelming sense of panic. Many of *Jeopardy!*'s most senior employees have worked on the show for decades; for some, it is the only workplace they've ever known.

And while there are plenty of other game shows out there, there is only one *Jeopardy!*: Nowhere else can you find a show that treats trivia and knowledge so reverentially, *and* produces more than two hundred episodes every single season, *and* has *Jeopardy!*'s air of legitimacy and cultural standing. In the eyes of many *Jeopardy!* employees, the show is not simply a job—it's a way of life.

Here, then, was the first real threat to the show. If fans of *Jeopardy!* were outraged by the revelations about Richards, those feelings were dramatically sharpened on set.

Richards began the meeting by repeating parts of the statement Sony had released on his behalf the previous day, which concluded: "My responsibilities today as a father, husband, and a public personality who speaks to many people through my role on television means I have substantial and serious obligations as a role model, and I intend to live up to them." And then Richards asked if anyone in the room had any questions.

Multiple longtime staffers stood up, laying out the confusion, anger, and now sadness that had defined their last year. One expressed outrage that Richards had destroyed their life's work.

Eventually, the meeting broke up, and the people who make *Jeopardy!* went back to doing what they have done for so long, recording a fresh slate of contestants fighting for the chance to be named a *Jeopardy!* champion.

And then they went home, uncertain of what would become of the show or their position at it. Some worried that the public confrontation would mean they had to leave jobs they had held for years. Others wondered how the show they loved could continue under the leadership of a person who seemed to be the antithesis of the thoughtful and caring man who had been the face and soul of the show across the previous four decades.

By the next morning, Sony announced that Richards would no longer be *Jeopardy!*'s host.

Eleven days later, he was done as executive producer too.

⟵

When I first began to write this book, *Jeopardy!* was at the precipice of change.

For thirty-six years, *Jeopardy!* had been a stalwart, rewarding its millions of fans with five nights of no-nonsense trivia each week.

The only alterations came at the margins: an occasional set redesign, flashes of peppier and poppier writing, and a salt-and-pepper host who had become, gradually but emphatically, gray.

Otherwise, it was the same show it had always been, with sixty-one clues, three hidden Daily Double chances, one final bit of wagering at the end, and a trio of razor-sharp contestants.

But it was clear that change was coming all the same—on camera and off. The streaming era and a growing legion of cord-cutters had imperiled network TV as a whole, eating away at the vaunted quiz show's ratings and raising questions about how *Jeopardy!* would adapt and lure younger audiences. A new generation of contestants had begun to rigorously analyze strategic advantages in wagering and clue selection, harbingers of a *Moneyball*-like statistical revolution that changed the way the game was being played. And, from Friedman on down, a behind-the-scenes changing of the guard loomed as well.

Ahead of his exit from the show, even Friedman seemed to be bracing for change. "The veterans on the staff know how lucky we are," he wrote in a 2014 email to a Sony executive that was revealed in that year's hack of the studio. "And I have no doubt the younger staff will eventually and forever think of these times as the good old days."

Even expecting change, however, did little to dull the sheer shock of what came next. There was the raucous guest-host carousel, with hosts and fans alike campaigning for their favorites to get the job. The Richards saga. The addition of

Michael Davies, who took over as executive producer from Richards and publicly embraced *Jeopardy!* statistics with analytical player scorecards. The rise of new super-champions in Amodio and Amy Schneider.

I'm often asked where I think *Jeopardy!* will go from here. If nothing else, I've been convinced that guessing the answer is a fool's errand. (For the last time, in the form of a question: *What is "no clue"?*)

But what has stood out most in this age of change is this: The core of it all is still intact.

Trebek often said that he wasn't the star of *Jeopardy!*—that honor, he insisted, belonged to the contestants. Even as a fan of the show—and an eager couch player who's had the fortune to meet many of those contestants—I don't think I ever really believed him. He was *Jeopardy!*'s epicenter for decades, and as I sat down to write this book, I worried how it could ever go on without him.

I've been proven resoundingly incorrect.

While the road has had bumps, *Jeopardy!* is thriving in every conceivable way: Its ratings are up, its fans are enthralled, and its would-be contestants are applying in record numbers.

The show will never be exactly what it was under Trebek, but he was right—the star power rested not with him but with the three people across the stage on any given night. And it rests, too, just offstage with the staff and crew, who have worked for decades to make *Jeopardy!* exactly what it is.

Trebek, as always, was the guy with all the answers.

ACKNOWLEDGMENTS

I can scarcely put into words my gratitude to the many, many, many members of the greater *Jeopardy!* community—past contestants, aspiring players, loyal fans, and everything in between—who made time to tell me about their experiences, answered my questions, made the mistake of inviting me to pub trivia, and explained to me why you should definitely use the enable light to determine buzzer timing and also why you should definitely not use the enable light to determine buzzer timing.

Many feature in this book's chapters by name, while others, just as vital, helped me build the scaffolding upon which those chapters are based. A few for whom I'm especially grateful: James Holzhauer, Fritz Holznagel, Bruce Lou, Pam Mueller, Brad Rutter, Mike Upchurch, Harvey Silikovitz, Lynn Yu, and the incomparable Ken Jennings, who was bafflingly generous with his time (not to mention his math and geography pointers). A special thanks to Buzzy Cohen, my *Jeopardy!* consigliere, to the tireless archivists at the J! Archive, and to the great Andy Saunders, who always has the answer and saved me more times than I can count. This book would not have been possible without your help.

Thank you to the *Jeopardy!* staff, past and present, for creating a wonderful game and an even better show; that this community has risen up around it is no coincidence.

Particular thanks go to the invaluable Alison Shapiro Cooke, who invited me onto the *Jeopardy!* set and let me spend days on end interrogating the staff.

To my editors and colleagues at *The Ringer*, especially Andrew Gruttadaro, who first encouraged me to cover *Jeopardy!* like a sport; Ben Glicksman, Chris Almeida, and Riley McAtee, who followed me all the way down the quiz show rabbit hole and helped me—finally—make some sense of it all; Bill Simmons, Mallory Rubin, and Sean Fennessey, who believed it could be fashioned into a book; my early readers, especially Andrea Rowan; Mark Hinog, *Jeopardy!* hypeman extraordinaire; and all the friends and family members who supported me through this process—Dad and Jill, Bo, Belinda and Mark, Cliff and Donna, Alex, and my brilliant mother, who first instilled a daily *Jeopardy!* habit—I cannot thank you enough.

To the fantastic folks at Twelve and Hachette—Sean Desmond and Rachel Kambury, as well as Estefania Acquaviva, Bob Castillo, Laura Jorstad, Zohal Karimy, Brian McLendon, Marie Mundaca, Megan Perritt-Jacobson, Eric Rayman, Paul Samuelson, Morgan Swift, Jarrod Taylor, and all the others who did the actual book-fashioning—thank you for your wisdom, your patience, and your beautiful work. Thanks also to the Gernert family and my agent, Sarah Bolling, who is directly responsible for the passage from our initial "what is a book?" conversation to what you see here.

Finally, to Justin, who planned our whole wedding while I was in the thick of this book (only for the wedding to be canceled due to the global pandemic two weeks out, on the very day this book was due): You are my favorite writer, my favorite reader, my all-around favorite and my love, and I'm so excited to wait out all the rain delays of life with you.

ABOUT THE AUTHOR

CLAIRE MCNEAR covers sports and culture for *The Ringer* and lives in Washington, DC. This is her first book.